COMMUNAL SOCIETIES IN AMERICA
AN AMS REPRINT SERIES

THE
CONSTITUTION
of
THE UNITED SOCIETIES,
OF BELIEVERS (CALLED SHAKERS)

AMS PRESS
NEW YORK

THE
CONSTITUTION
of
THE UNITED SOCIETIES,
OF BELIEVERS (CALLED SHAKERS)

CONTAINING

SUNDRY COVENANTS AND ARTCLES OF AGREMENT, DEFINITIVE OF THE LEGAL GROUNDS OF THE INSTITUTION.

"Wisdom hath builded her house"—   SOLOMON
And—"Other foundation can no man lay".—   PAUL.

WATERVLIET, (OHIO)
1833

Library of Congress Cataloging in Publication Data
Shakers.
 The constitution of the United Societies of Believers (called Shakers).

 (Communal societies in America)
 Reprint of the 1833 ed. published in Watervliet, Ohio.
 1. Shakers   I. Title.
 BX9776.S48   1978   289.8   72-2992
 ISBN 0-404-10754-0

First AMS edition published in 1978.

Reprinted from the edition of 1833, Watervliet, Ohio. [Trim size of the original has been slightly altered in this edition. Original trim size: 11.2 × 19.7 cm. Text area of the original has been maintained.]

MANUFACTURED
IN THE UNITED STATES OF AMERICA

AN EXPLANATORY NOTE AND LISTING OF CONTENTS TO THE AMS EDITION

This publication exists in several different forms. We have compiled what we believe is the most complete version, utilizing microfilmed copies from Williams College (Williamstown, Mass.) and the Library of Congress. Material duplicated in the originals has been eliminated in this edition. A listing of contents follows, to assist the reader. [For a detailed discussion of this title, the reader is referred to the excellent *Shaker Literature: A Bibliography,* compiled and edited by M. L. Richmond, vol. 1, pp. 126–127 (entry no. 911).]

Sundry Covenants &c. Copy of the first Covenant in Ohio, drafted by Elder Benjamin, and executed in the year 1810. pp. [1]–2.

A Brief Exposition of the Established Principles, and Regulations of the United Society of Believers called Shakers. Printed at Albany, 1830; and now reprinted, with sundry improvements suggested by the Author . . . Watervliet, Ohio, 1832. [36 pp.]

An Improved Edition of the Church Covenant, or Constitution of the United Societies, called Shakers. (Dayton, Ohio, 1833). pp. [37]–48.

The Covenant, or Constitution of the Church, at Union-Village, Ohio. pp. [62]–72.

The Constitution, or Covenant of the Church, at Pleasant-Hill. (Kentucky). pp. [61]–72.

Circular Epistle. pp. [73]–80.

The Church-Covenant, Executed at Union-Village, January 15th 1812. The State of Ohio Warren County. pp. [81]–88.

The Church-Covenant, Executed at Pleasant-Hill June 2nd, 1814. The State of Kentucky Mercer County. pp. [81]–84.

The Church-Covenant, Executed at Watervliet December 7th 1818. State of Ohio Montgomery County. pp. [89]–96.

General Rules of the United Society, and Summary Articles of Mutual Agreement and Release. (Watervliet, Montgomery County, Ohio, January 1833.) pp. [3]–9.

A Revision and Confirmation of the Social Compact of the United Society called Shakers, at Pleasant-Hill, Kentucky. (Harrodsburg, Ky. 1830). pp. [1]–12.

Investigator, or a Defense of the Order, Governmennt & Economy of the United Society called Shakers . . . .Pleasant-Hill, Ky. [8 pp.] pp. [11]–47.

A Special Covenant of the First Family of the Church dated 3rd Month 8th 1815. [2 pp.]

SUNDRY COVENANTS &c.

Copy of the first Covenant in Ohio, drafted by Elder Benjamin, and executed in the year 1810.

WHEREAS we the subscribers, near Lebanon, in the township of Turtlecreek, county of Warren and state of Ohio, and members of the community of people known by the name of *Shakers*; believing that Christ hath made his Second Appearance, to make an end of sin, and that he has begun to establish his kingdom of everlasting righteousness and peace, on earth, which is free to all people, (who will receive it) and will stand forever: And whereas we, having by the grace of God, through faith and obedience, been made partakers of the gospel of salvation, by which we are called to take up our cross daily, and follow Christ in the regeneration—to renounce the union and relation of the flesh, and instead thereof, to labor for the union & relation of the Spirit, by which, according to the promise of God made known in this day, He will gather together, in one, all things in Christ, which are in heaven and upon earth: And whereas we feel it to be our duty and privilege, to obey the call of God by the gospel; and being desirous to live the remainder of our time on earth, in that manner in which we can do the most good, for the honor of God, for the increse and support of the gospel, and for the mutual comfort and happiness of each other, and the benefit of mankind,— And being united in willingness to declare our faith & and the reason of our proceedings, as matter of conscience and choice, and not of fraud nor compulsion,— And for an end of all controversy to those whom it may afterwards concern, *Therefore*, according to our own faith and desire, and of our free-will and voluntary choice, we mutually covenant and agree, to live together in one family, now under the spiritual care of David Darrow, & on the premises belonging to the joint-interest of the Church of our community; and to this intent, as brethren and sisters in the gospel of our only Lord and Savior Jesus Christ, we do severally and jointly, freely and voluntarily covenant and agree to devote, use and improve our interest, our time, our strength and our talents, for the mutual benefit, support and comfor of each other, for the support and furtherance of the gospel, for the good of the widow and fatherless, and such as may be deemed real objects of charity, and for any other pious & charitable uses which the gospel may require.

And we do, by these presents, severally and jointly, of our own free choice, and by our own voluntary act, solemnly & conscientiously, covenant and agree, never to bring any debt, blame or demand whatever, against the said David or any other member or members of said family, or against any other person or persons of our community, on account of any labor or service that has been or may be done by us, or any of us, severally or jointly;— particular agreements, in writing, between members of different families are hereby only excepted.

And we do further agree, and it is hereby expressly understood & provided, that when any one or more of us shall see cause to move from this family to any other family of the communiy or to withdraw from the community, we shall be at full liberty so todo, and to take with us our property, if any we have brought in.

But provided, in all cases (the original property of individuals excepted) that we shall leave each other free from all debt, blame, or demand whatsoever.

In testimony whereof we, both brethren and sisters, have hereunto set our hands, in presence of each other, this 14th day of March, A. D. 1810.

David Darrow, Daniel Mosely, Solomon King, Peter Pease, Archibald Meacham, Benjamin S. Youngs, Issachar Bates, Elisha Dennis, Barachah Dennis, Ross Morrell, James Hodge, Nathan Sharp, Henry Morrell John Carson, Joseph Lockwood.

Ruth Farrington, Molly Goodrich, Ruth Darrow Lucy Bacon, Rachel Johnson, Hortency Goodrich Martha Sanford, Edith Dennis, Eunice Bedle, Caty Rubart, Susanna Liddil Polly Thomas, Jenny M'Nemar Polly Davis, Hannah Carson Rachel Duncan, Rachel Dennis, Phebe Lockwood,

A
BRIEF EXPOSITION

OF THE ESTABLISHED

PRINCIPLES, AND REGULATIONS

OF THE

UNITED SOCIETY OF BELIEVERS

CALLED SHAKERS.

Printed at Albany, in the year 1830; and now reprinted, with sundry improvements suggested by the Author.

"*O magna vis veritatis ! Cic.*"

The power of truth is great,
It must and will prevail,
When false reports shall cease,
And sland'rous tongues shall fail.

WATERVLIET, OHIO.

1832.

THIS small publication has a twofold object. First, to exhibit the people commonly called Shakers, in their proper character, as citizens of the commonwealth, and under the influence and operation of its laws. In this view, it is presented to the statesman, whether legislator, lawyer, judge, or jurist. Second, to solve the many questions proposed by the religious world, concerning these singular people, as a religious community. For this purpose, it is offered to the professors of religion, of all societies, & all candid inquirers.

The EXPOSITION, *in its first form, was hastily written for the purpose of obviating a defamatory bill presented to the legislature of New York: It is now somewhat abridged, in order to comprise, in few words, the main points in question, and afford room for a more full and free discussion of those points, which, to the intelligent and candid Reader, will, no doubt, be both edifying and entertaining.*

―――――

A BRIEF EXPOSITION, &c.

Many erroneous opinions are entertained concerning the people generally known by the name of Shakers, which are calculated to mislead the public mind, in respect to the true character of this *Society*. Many false reports and incorrect statements have been circulated respecting our principles and practice, which have no foundation in truth. With a view to correct these erroneous opinions, and as far as in our power, to remove prejudices and false impressions, we are induced, from a sense of duty, to lay before the candid public a brief statement of facts respecting the principles, government, temporal order, and practical regulations of the Society. This duty we owe to ourselves and to our fellow creatures, for the correct information of the public, and the benefit of all concerned: that all who are governed by the spirit of candor, and wish to know the truth concerning us, may no longer depend on the vague and inconsistent reports in circulation, from which they can gain no correct knowledge nor just information.

Altho we have published considerable respecting our principles and rules of association; yet an opinion seems still to prevail, especially among strangers, that no person can be admitted as a member of the Society without first surrendering all his temporal property, & wholly divesting himself of the government of his family & the care of his children, if he have any, and subjecting himself and all that he possesses to the arbitrary control of the Elders and leaders of the Society. Nothing can be more erroneous and incorrect than such a supposition. Those things are no more required to obtain admission into this Society than into any other. We believe that no institution, nor any system of government could be established which would be more compatible with man's free agency, or more consistent with truth, justice, reason, and all our national rights civil and religious, than the system that we have adopted. The following primary principles constitute the basis on which this Society is founded, and by which all its movements and operations are directed.

§ I. FAITH AND PRINCIPLES OF THE SOCIETY.

1. A life of *innocence* and *purity*, according to the example of Jesus Christ and his first true followers; implying entire abstinence from all sensual and carnal gratifications.

2. LOVE.— "By this shall all men know that ye are my disciples if ye have love one to another. Love is the fulfilling of the law." This is our bond of union.

3. PEACE.— "Follow peace with all men," is a divine precept; hence our abstinence from war and bloodshed, from all acts of violence towards our fellow men, from all the party contentions and politics of the world, and from all the pursuits of pride and worldly ambition. "My kingdom [said Christ] is not of this world."

4. JUSTICE.— "Render to every man his due. Owe no man any thing, but to love one another." We are to be just and honest in all our dealings with mankind, to discharge all just dues, duties, and equitable claims, as seasonably and effectually as possible.

5. HOLINESS,— "without which no man shall see the

Lord." Which signifies to be *consecrated*, or set apart from a common to a sacred use. Hence arises all our doctrines and practical rules of dedicating our persons, services, and property to social and sacred uses, having adopted the example of the first gospel Church, in establishing & supporting one *consecrated & united* interest by the voluntary choice of every member, as a sacred privilege, and not by any undue constraint or persuasion.

6. GOODNESS. Do good to all men, as far as opportunity and ability may serve, by administering acts of charity and kindness, and promoting light and truth among mankind. "Whatsoever ye would that men should do to you, do ye even so to them."

7. TRUTH. This principle is opposed to falsehood, lying, deceit, and hypocrisy; and implies fidelity, reality, good earnest, sincerity, and punctuality in keeping vows and promises. These principles are the genuine basis of our institution, planted by its first founders, exhibited in all our public writings, justified by scripture and fair reason, and practically commended as a system of morality and religion, adapted to the best interest and happiness of man, both here and hereafter.

§ II. OF ADMITTING MEMBERS.

It must be obvious to every reasonable person, that the foregoing principles are, in many respects, very contrary to the carnal and selfish nature of fallen man, and doubtless more so than those of any other religious society. Therefore there is little danger to be apprehended of any person's being flattered or inveigled into this Society, or of joining it from any other motive than purely from the operations of faith & conscience. This of itself is the most powerful guard that can be set against the deceptions so often reported to be practised by the Society in procuring members. Indeed it precludes the possibility of such deceptions to any alarming extent. To this it may be truly added, that all reasonable precaution is used against admitting any person to membership while ignorant of our real faith and principles, or of the following *General Rules*.

1. All persons who unite with us, in any degree, must do it freely and voluntarily, according to their own faith and unbiassed judgment.

2. In our testimony, both public and private, no flattery, nor any undue influence is used; but the most plain and explicit statements of our faith and principles are laid before the inquirer; so that the whole ground may be comprehended, as far as possible, by every candidate for admission.

3. No considerations of property are ever made use of, to induce any person to join us, nor to prevent any one from leaving us; because it is our faith, that no act of devotion or service that does not flow from the free and voluntary emotions of the heart, can be acceptable to God as an act of true religion.

4. No believing husband or wife is allowed, by our rules, to separate from an unbelieving partner, except by mutual agreement; unless the conduct of the unbeliever be such as to warrant a separation by the laws of the land. Nor can any husband or wife who has otherwise abandoned his or her partner, be received into communion with the Society.

5. Any person becoming a member must rectify all his wrongs, and, as fast and as far as it is in his power, discharge all just and legal claims, whether of creditors or filial heirs. Nor can any person, not conforming to this rule, long remain in union with the Society. But the Society is not responsible for the debts of any individual, except by agreement; because such responsibility would involve a principle ruinous to the institution.

6. No difference is to be made in the distribution of parental estate among the heirs, whether they belong to the society or not; but an equal partition must be made as far as may be practicable and consistent with reason and justice.

7. If an unbelieving wife separate from a believing husband, by agreement, the husband must give her a just and reasonable share of the property; and if they have children who have arrived to years of understanding sufficient to judge for themselves, and who chuse to go with their mother, they are not to be disinherited

on that account. Tho the character of this institution has been much censured on this ground; yet we boldly assert that the rule above stated has never, to our knowledge, been violated by this Society.

8. Industry, temperance, and frugality are prominent features of this institution. No member who is able to labor, can be permitted to live idly upon the labors of others. All are required to be employed in some manual occupation, according to their several abilities, when not engaged in other necessary duties.

§ III.   MANNER OF GOVERNMENT.

It must be obvious to every reflecting mind, that the government of this Society cannot be of a tyrannical & arbitrary character. Nor can any government which is not just & equitable in itself, long exist in it; because the faith and principles of the Society can support no other, as no government can be maintained in it, but by the faith and general approbation of the members: besides, the liberal principles held forth in the constitutions and general laws of the land, would be an insurmountable barrier to a government of any other character And even if this barrier were insufficient, it is well known that the world presents to the view of the natural mind, enjoyments much more pleasing than those contained in the rules of this Society. It would therefore be impossible for a government, which should prove itself tyrannical, and exercise unjust powers, ever to sway the faith of the members, and shut the avenues to the world, so as to prevent them from withdrawing, and seeking the more naturally pleasing enjoyments which it affords.

The rules of government in the Society are adapted to the different orders of which it is composed. In all (as far as respects adults) it is spiritual, its powers and authorities growing out of the *mutual faith, love, and confidence* of all the members, and harmoniously concurring in the general form and manner of government established by the first founders of the Society.

1. The effective basis of the government so established, and which is the support of all its institutions, is

the faith, voluntary choice, union and general approbation of the members. It is an established maxim in the Society, that any member who is not reconciled to the faith, order, and government established in it, is more injurious than beneficial to it; besides the loss to himself of his own time and privilege; therefore, whenever this is found to be the case with any one, and he continues in that situation, he is advised peaceably to withdraw. As all who unite with this Society do it voluntarily, and can at any time withdraw, they are in duty bound to submit to its government. All are required by the rules of the Society to do this, or withdraw; and this we think is reasonable, as no body of people can exist in any associated capacity, unless such power be maintained in its government.

2. The first leading gift in the Society is vested in a Ministry, generally consisting of four persons, including both sexes. It belongs to the Ministry to appoint Elders and Trustees. These, in union with the Ministry, constitute the general government of the Society in all its branches; and being supported by the general union and approbation of the members, are invested with power to appoint their successors and other subordinate officers, as occasion may require; to counsel, advise and direct in all matters, whether of a spiritual or temporal nature; to superintend the concerns of the several families, and establish all needful orders, rules, & regulations for the direction and protection of the several branches of the Society; but no rule can be made, nor any member assume a lead, contrary to the original faith & known principles of the Society. And nothing which respects the government, order and general arrangement of the Society, is considered as fully established, until it has received the general approbation of the Society, or of that branch of it which it more immediately concerns.

3. No creed can be framed to limit the progress of improvement. It is the faith of the society, that the operations of divine light are unlimited All are at liberty to improve their talents and exercise their gifts, the younger being subject to the elder, and all in concert with the general lead.

4. In the order and government of the Society no corporal punishment is approved, nor any external force or violence exercised on any member. *Faith, Conscience,* or *Reason* is sufficient to influence a rational being; but where these are wanting, the necessary and proper means of restraint are not prohibited.

5. The management of temporal affairs, in families holding a united interest, as far as respects the consecrated property of the Society, is committed to Trustees. These are appointed by the Ministry and Elders; and being supported as aforesaid, are legally invested with the fee of the real estate belonging to the Society.

All the consecrated property comes under their general charge, together with the oversight of all public business, & all commercial dealings without the bounds of the community. But all the transactions of the Trustees, in the use, management, and disposal of this united interest must be done in behalf, and for the joint benefit of the Society, and not for any personal or private use or purpose whatever. And in all these things, they are strictly responsible to the general lead of the Society for the faithful performance of their duty.

It is also an established principle, that no Trustee, nor any member whatever, shall contract debts of any kind, in behalf of the Society.

§ IV. ORDER AND ARRANGEMENT OF THE SOCIETY.

THIS community, is divided into several different branches, commonly called families- This division is generally made for the sake of convenience, and is often rendered necessary on account of local situation and occurrent circumstances; but the proper division and arrangement of the community, without respect to local situation is into three classes, or progressive degrees of order, as follows:

1. The first, or novitiate class, are those who receive our faith, and come into a degree of relation, but chuse to live in their own family order, and manage their own temporal concerns. Any who chuse, may live in that order, and be owned as brethren and sisters in the gospel, so long as they live up to its requirements

Parents are to be kind and dutiful to each other, to shun every appearance of evil, provide for their family, bring up their children in a godly manner, use, improve and dispose of their property wisely, and manage their affairs according to their own discretion. They may thus continue as long as it comports with their faith, their circumstances, and their spiritual improvement. But they are required to bear in mind the necessity and importance of a spiritual increase, without which they are ever exposed to fall back into the course and spirit of the world; and they can hold their connection with the Society, only so long as they continue to conform to its religious faith and principles.

Such persons are admitted to all the privileges in the Society spiritual or temporal, necessary to give them a full understanding of all that they wish to know. No control is exercised, by the Society, over their persons, property, nor children; but being members of a religious society, they are to be subject to the spiritual direction of their leaders, and may receive counsel in temporal matters, whenever they feel it necessary to apply. If at any time they desire to make a donation to any religious or charitable purpose of the Society, they are at liberty to do so; provided they be clear of debt, and their circumstances will otherwise admit of it; but after having freely made the donation, they can have no more right to reclaim it, than the members of other religious societies have to reclaim the like donations.

The education and government of children belonging to this class, is an important object. Where the number of private families is sufficient, they may establish a school, and jointly contribute to the support of it, and in this way dispose of their property for the joint benefit of their posterity; but if any have estates, they may reserve them, in whole or in part, for the benefit of their children when they become of age.

No children are ever taken under the immediate charge of the Society, except with the free consent of all parties. But few comparatively are admitted.

Those taken into the Society are treated with care and tenderness, receive a good school education, according to genius, are trained to industry and virtuous habits, restrained from vice, and at a suitable age, led into the knowledge of the Sacred Scriptures, & practically taught the divine precepts contained in them, particularly those of Jesus Christ and the Apostles.

2. The second, or junior class, is composed of persons who, not having the charge of families, and being under no embarrassments to hinder them from uniting together in community order, chuse to enjoy the benefits of that situation. These (for mutual safety) enter into a contract to devote their services, freely, to support the interest of the family of which they are members, so long as they continue in that order; stipulating, at the same time, to claim no pecuniary compensation for their services. But all the members of such families are mutually benefitted by the united interest and labors of the whole family, so long as they continue to support the order thereof; and they are amply provided for in health, sickness, and old age. These benefits are secured to them by contract.

Members of this class or order have the privilege, at their option, by contract, to give the improvement of any part or all of their property, to be freely used for the mutual benefit of the family to which they belong. The property itself may be resumed at any time, according to the contract; but no interest can be claimed for the use thereof; nor can any member of such family be employed therein for wages of any kind. Members of this order may retain the lawful ownership of all their own property as long as they think it proper, and chuse so to do; but at any time, after having sufficient experience, to be able to act deliberately and understandingly, they may, if they chuse, dedicate and devote a part or the whole, and consecrate it forever, to the support of the institution. But this is a matter of free choice; we urge no one to do so, but they are rather advised, in such cases, to consider the matter well, so as not to do it until they have a full understanding of its consequences; lest they should do it prematurely, and afterwards repent of it.

3. The third, or *Senior* class is composed of such per-

sons as have had sufficient time and opportunity practically to prove our faith and manner of life, and are thus prepared to enter fully, freely and voluntarily, into a united and consecrated interest. These, solemnly, covenant and agree to dedicate and devote themselves and services, with all that they possess, to the service of God and the support of the gospel forever, solemnly promising never to bring debt, nor damage, claim nor demand against the Society, nor against any member thereof, for any property or service which they have thus devoted to the uses and purposes of the institution.

To enter fully into this order, is considered by the Society to be a matter of the utmost importance to the parties concerned, and therefore requires the most mature and deliberate consideration; for after having made such a dedication, according to the laws of justice and equity there can be no ground for retraction. Nor can they by those laws, recover any thing whatever which has been thus dedicated. Of this all are fully apprised before entering into the contract. Yet should any afterward withdraw, and be disappointed in their worldly prospects, the society may charitably supply their wants as a matter of grace, but not of debt, nor to support them in idleness and dissipation. No person who withdraws peaceably is sent away empty.

During a period of more than forty years, since the permanent establishment of this Society, at New-Lebanon and Watervliet, there never has been a legal claim entered, by any person, for the recovery of property brought into the Society; but all claims of that nature, if any have existed, have been amicably settled to the satisfaction of the parties concerned. Complaints and legal prosecutions have not, hitherto, come from persons who brought property into the Institution; but from those who came destitute of property, and who, generally speaking have been no benefit to the Society, in any way; but on the contrary, after having enjoyed its hospitality, and brought no small share of trouble upon the people, have had the assurance to lay claim to wages which they never earned, or property to which they never had any just nor legal claim.

No person can be received into this order until he shall have settled all just and legal claims, both of creditors and filial heirs; so that whatever property he may possess, may be justly and truly his own. Minors cannot be admitted as covenant members of this order; yet they may be received under its immediate care and protection. And when they shall have arrived at lawful age, if they should chuse to continue in the Society, and sign the covenant of the order, and support its principles, they are then admitted to all the privileges of members. The members of this order are all equally entitled to the benefits and privileges thereof, without any difference made on account of what any one may have contributed to the interest of the Society. All are equally entitled to their support and maintenance, and to every necessary comfort, whether in health, sickness or old age, so long as they continue to maintain the principles, and conform to the orders, rules and regulations of the institution. They therefore give their property and services for the most valuable of all temporal considerations; an ample security, during life, for every needful support, if they continue faithful to their contract and covenant, the nature of which they clearly understand before they enter into it.

It may readily be seen, that such an order could not be supported, if its members, on withdrawing, should take whatever they have given, and have the avails of their labors restored to them. They have agreed to give it all to sacred and charitable purposes, claiming nothing but their own support from it. It has been disposed of according to their own desire; and the institution may therefore be no better able to refund it, than if such dedication had never been made. If therefore, it should be returned to them, it would be literally taking it from those who remain faithful to their covenant, and giving it to covenant breakers. Who cannot see that this would be both unreasonable and unjust?

Notwithstanding all reports to the contrary, we confidently assert that no person has been wronged, by any dedication of property ever made to the purposes of this Society; and that no person whatever, has any just or reasonable ground of complaint in this respect,

B

This Society [New Lebanon] has served as a pattern for all the societies or branches of the community which have been established in various parts of the United States. In every place where the faith & testimony of the Society has been planted, the same orders and rules of government have been gradually established & maintained; so that the Society and its members are now generally known; and from the striking peculiarities which distinguish them from all other societies, no person need be deceived by impostors.

The perpetuity of the Society is the last thing to be considered, on which we offer the following remarks.

We believe it will be generally granted, that the history of the world does not furnish a single instance of any religious institution, which has stood fifty years without a visible declension of the principles of the institution in the general purity and integrity of its members. This has been generally acknowledged by the devotees of such institutions, and facts have fully verified it. But we would appeal to the candid judgment of those who have known this institution from the beginning, and have had a fair opportunity of observing the progress of its improvement, whether they have, in reality, found any declension, either in the external order and regulations of the Society, or in the purity and integrity of its members, in the general practice of the moral and christian duties; and whether they have not, on the contrary, discovered a visible and manifest increase in all these respects. And hence they may judge for themselves, whether the moral character of the society, and its progressive improvement, can be ascribed to any other cause than the blessing, protection and government of Divine Power and Wisdom; and why its perpetuity should be called in question.

Published in behalf of the Society, by

CALVIN GREEN } Cmmittee
and } of
SETH Y. WELLS, } Publication.

New-Lebanon, March 15th, 1830.

THE EXPOSITION CONTINUED,

In answer to sundry inquiries and objections.

PREAMBLE.— *In the year* 1828, *a pamphlet was published by the Believers in Kentucky, entitled* "THE INVESTIGATOR, *or a defence of the order, government, &c. of the United Society.—Addressed to the political world*".
Part of what was written on that occasion, by the committee of publication, being of a religious cast, it was retained for future consideration. The writer (D. Spining) *having been for a long time, an Elder in the junior order, & well apprised of the inquiries & objections of serious minds, had in view to treat the subject in a manner edifying to such. We had thought of printing the manuscript entire; but so much of the matter has been anticipated in the foregoing pages, that, to avoid repetition, we have selected such parts as may serve to answer the original design.*

NOTWITHSTANDING much has been published for the information of mankind, relative to the faith and practice of the United Society of Believers; yet we find many among the most candid and intelligent, who are still at a loss, and often anxiously and, we hope, honestly seeking further information, especially on matters of a practical nature, For the satisfaction of such, the following pages have been written; and as truth is our object, we shall aim at presenting it in so plain a dress that it may be easily comprehended by persons of common capacity.

In the first place; it is a question with many, whether this Society has for its primary object the things of this world, or that which is to come. This question is, of all others, of the greatest importance, and ought to be first settled. It is strangely supposed, that if our main object were to prepare for a future state, we would show a greater indifference about the things of time; but instead of this, that we are as zealous to provide a good living, and to have every thing about us in the best order, and of the most durable quality: hence we have been puplicly denounced, as "a set of worldly minded, cunning deceivers."

To this strange kind of reasoning we need only reply; that all our zeal in improving temporal things, and, taking satisfaction in the enjoyment of them, will not prove that we have no greater enjoyments in prospect; and we think, that the manner in which we use temporal things, may serve as positive proof, that we consider them of but little value, in comparison with the things of eternity

Where is the man of the world that could be induced by any thing earthly, to confess all his most secret sins, and take up a full cross against all manner of sin and uncleanness in his knowledge, and live the life of selfdenial that we live? This single appeal may satisfy the conscience of any man, that nothing but motives purely religious can possibly induce any person to join this society, and perseveringly conform to its rules and orders.

1. *The confession of sins.* This being the initiating act, opens a large field of inquiry, and some weighty objections, especially among Protestants, who have imbibed such a disgust to almost every point of order held sacred by the Church of Rome. It is questioned whether the order of the gospel be, to confess to God alone, in general terms, or to name the particular acts, thing by thing, in the presence of witnesses appointed to hear, remit, and counsel, as the case may be.

The idea of confessing to man, or of any man having power to forgive sin, is generally viewed by Protestants as the greatest presumption. But were it not for the abuses of this sacred order, by the Catholic Church, no Protestant, nor any other person of candor, could read the scriptures attentively, and not see that an oral confession of sins, such as we have adopted, was practised both under the law and the gospel. The confession, if sincere, is indeed made to God, and it is by his order that the penitent is released, and his sins forgiven him. "Whose soever sins ye remit, they are remitted unto them, *and* whose soever ye retain, they are retained."

2. *Selfdenial* comes next in the order of things. The

remission of sins that are past only serves to place the candidate on the ground of further trial. By bringing his deeds to the light, he sees what kind of a creature he is, and what he shall do with himself is now the question. The answer is "Deny thyself." Can any thing be more objectionble? Self is the supreme object of every natural man; nothing so near and dear to him as himself; of course, to deny himself appears the greatest inconsistency imaginable. Hence it becomes a deep labor to reconcile the mind, in any degree to a course so directly opposite to that of nature.

The candidate, views and reviews his whole life, his actions, and his principles of action, and compares them with their opposites now set before him in the precepts of the gospel and the example of Believers; the infallible result of which, in every honest man, is selfabhorrence and a sincere inquiry, "Lord, what wilt thou have me to do?" Take up thy cross" is the answer.

3. *The Cross of Christ* comes next in order, which, in a figure, may be called a toll-gate, well described by the poet,—These holy gates forever bar
    Pollution sin and shame;
    None can obtain admittance there
    But followers of the Lamb.

Here is the grand halting place with the generality; here, let facts be fairly disclosed, and Newton gives us the result,—If Self must be deni'd,
    And sin forsaken quite,
    They rather chuse the way that's wide,
    And strive to think it right.

But to an honest soul there is no time to hesitate, no room for evasion or getting round the cross; no alternative but to make a full surrender, an entire sacrifice. It might, perhaps, be understood, that great latitude is given to the young Believer, to hold and manage his own property, family, &c. It is only so considered after the manner of men; the faith of the gospel makes no reserve. Whoever denies self, denies all that belongs to self The grand requisition to discipleship embraces "all that he hath" He is not his own, & what can he have that he can call his own?

Thus the honest soul, having received the faith of the gospel, confessed his sins, denied himself, and taken up his cross, is placed on the proper ground of probation, to follow Christ in the regeneration; which leads to a further inquiry into those several steps which are considered more or less objectionable, by the generality of mankind.

The first step, which the Believer takes in conformity to the example of Christ, is to withdraw from the communion and fellowship of the world.—"Two cannot walk together except they be agreed."

The disagreement between the spirit of Christ and the spirit of the world is irreconcilable: therefore, the first step that goes to test our faith, is prompt obedience to the call of Christ, which ever was, is, and ever will be, "Come ye out from among them, and be ye separate." Hence begins the first order of the Society.

No consideration of an earthly nature can bind the Believer to his former associates, or separate him from the company of those, to whom he is united in spirit.— The terms laid down by the Captain of our salvation are unalterable.—No worldly honor, no earthly interest, no natural affection is taken for an excuse; but whatever cannot be adjusted and disposed of in an orderly manner, must be forsaken.—"If any *man* come to me, and hate not his father, and mother, and wife and children, and brethren, and sisters, yea, and his own life also, he cannot be my disciple."—"He that loveth father or mother more than me, is not worthy of me; and he that loveth son or daughter more than me, is not worthy of me;—And he that taketh not his cross, and followeth after me, is not worthy of me." (Mat. 10. 37.)

We have no system of rules to prescribe the form and manner of proceeding, in this matter, each individual acts according to circumstances: If there be a neighborhood of Believers, they are under no necessity of selling or forsaking their houses or lands, or deserting their families.

They establish their own rules of operation, and unbelievers rarely mix with them, unless it is to persecute and afflict them. Any that live remote, if they are not driven off, may take their time for settling their temporal concerns, and moving within the bounds of the Society.—If they be single persons, they are accommodated in some of the families of Believers, those who have families move them somewhere near, if they be wiling to come, and provide for them if they be able; if not, they depend on their brethren for help.

When a family is divided, and part hold with the world, and part with the Believers, it furnishes occasion for many objections, which may all be answered in the words of Christ." I am come not to send peace, but rather division." (Luke 12, 51.)

2. When thus separated from the world, and located in society order, the next step is to test their union and relation to each other. Their first faith was to make a full and unreserved surrender to God, and it now remains to prove the sincerity of their dedication. If God is in heaven and we upon earth, how is he to receive this dedication and surrender? This question is answered by Christ himself; Whatsoever ye do unto the least of these my brethren ye do it unto me.

The matter then is to regulate and adjust the general interest to the best advantage for the mutual support and benefit of all. This is a radical principle that pervades the whole concern from its embryo, to its greatest maturity, and holds a selfish nature to the cross in every arrangement that takes place.

The arrangement of persons, is a matter of the first importance, to organize them in family order, to assign to each individual the lot and place which he is best qualified to fill, and in which he can improve his talents to the best advantage. This, however wise and economical, is not without serious objections, particularly on the ground of disorganizing families, and dissolving the ties of nature. But so it is, that gospel relation has to be gained, tho it be at the expense of those partial affections so highly prized by the children of this world.

3. When a family, in gospel relation, is thus constituted, the next inquiry is, what step is taken to arrange their temporal interest and their mutual labors, so as to prevent confusion? What example has Christ given in

that respect? Answer. In the first gathering of Believers, under the ministry of the Apostles, while they had all things common, there was cause of murmuring, till deacons were appointed to see that justice was done to all. According to this example, when joint property is appropriated to common purposes, it is placed under the care and management of a deaconship, who are to be responsible for the same.

A covenant is entered into between the parties, in which the use and benefit of the property and the services of all and each are freely devoted to the common support of the family; but to prevent fraud or imposition, no transfer of property is made to the deacon or any other person.

As this order is merely probationary, the utmost caution is used to avoid imposition. Each who brings property with him, has it valued by disinterested men, takes an inventory of it signed by the appraisers, delivers it to the care and custody of the deacon, and if he should afterwards call for it, he receives it without interest, & gives a receit and acquittance from all further demands.

The reasons for retaining this joint property on the ground of individual and separate claims is, to afford each a sufficient time of trial, and to secure a just settlement of all individual accounts. As long as there is any ground of claim upon the individual, his property remains in his own power, liable for his debts and other personal purposes. It is therefore in this order that all matters are adjusted relating to property, all accounts settled with creditors, and donations given or appropriations made to heirs: But above every temporal consideration, it is here that the following lines are realized;— Our flesh and sense must be deni'd,
Passion and envy, lust and pride;
While justice, temp'rance truth & love
Our inward piety approve.*

Few objections are ever got up against the order of such a family, relative to their domestic economy; but the case of the withdrawing member sometimes excites the tender sympathies of the world.—For such to receive barely what they brought in; no interest; no wages!

* Dr. Watts.

How will this comport with the injunctions of scripture, not to defraud the hireling of his wages; or how will it bear the scrutiny of the laws of the land?

Answer. We have ever, from the beginning, discarded the idea of hireing each other, or paying wages to any member of the Society; therefore no objection can arise on the ground of defrauding a hireling; and as for paying interest, it is pointedly prohibited by the moral law.

"Thou shalt not lend upon usury to thy brother, usury of money, usury of victuals, usury of any thing that is lent upon usury."—"Lord who shall abide in thy tabernacle? Who shall dwell in thy holy hill?" Mark the answer.—"He that putteth not out his money to usury."

As for the laws of the land, they will be considered hereafter, in reference to a higher order, which is the next subject of inquiry.

3. The third and last step that is marked out for our journey through time, is into Church order, where the spirits of men are to be tried as by fire, their characters fairly tested, and their destiny decided for a future state.

Short of this order, individuals may pass in and out, but whoever advances into Church relation, may calculate to go out no more. He enters this order as Noah entered the ark, to ride the foaming billows of time, and terminate his voyage on the peaceful shores of eternity.

To this ark of safety, the true Believer steadily and gradually progresses, making strait paths for his feet, until he arrives at the door of admission.

When a competent number have passed thro' a sufficient trial of their faith in the junior order, and are unitedly prepared to establish and support Church relation, they have only to ratify and confirm their inward agreement by executing what is, by way of eminence, called the Church Covenant, the entire form of which, has never as yet, been published to the world; we shall therefore only state the outlines of its stipulations.

The parties solemnly announce their faith, and the object of their associating together in that order.

They agree to live together as brethren and sisters of *one family*, possessing *one consecrated interest*, and equally enjoying the benefits of the same; to conform to the order of the Church heretofore known and approved.—The several orders of Ministry, Elders, Deacons, and Trustees, and the duties of each are severally designated, as also the duties and obligations, rights and privileges of the members respectively. They further, in the most explicit terms relinquish all claim to personal or private property, and wages for their services, and debar, not only themselves, but their heirs and assigns forever, from all private claims to the said consecrated interest, on account of any property or service which they may have contributed and bestowed, and jointly securing to all and each, the unmolested enjoyment of all those benefits and privileges, spiritual and temporal during life, provided they perseveringly conform to the principles and rules of the institution.

The visible fruits of the Senior order are the best comment on its principles. The world have little to say but in admiration. Nor would the most penetrating eye discover, in all the arrangement, cause for complaint, cr criminal charge, without the help of a Judas, to misrepresent & falsify.

No trouble or calamity, worth naming has ever arisen on this consecrated ground, but through the agency and instrumentality of those who violate their sacred engagements, renounce the faith, and demand reparation, for the damages which they pretend they have sustained.

But, as this is a subject of peculiar importance, we shall give it a distinct consideration.

THE CLAIMS OF WITHDRAWING MEMBERS CONSIDERED.

The case now under consideration having been briefly treated in the preceding part of this work, we shall continue the inquiry, under a general appeal to every rule of right, and see whether on any fair principle the community can be made liable for property so devoted, or labor performed under such conditions.

Let us then, in the first place, inquire: Is it just and right to retain such donations, in the eye of the law?

The answer is clear, that if the law grants the liberty of bestowing a gift, it never can revoke the gift made under the sanction of that law; since all the blessings of a free government depend on the protection of life, liberty, and the enjoyment of property; the right of using property righteously acquired must, of course, be accounted one of its blessings. We boast of our Constitution and it expressly prohibits the enacting of any law which would impair any *bona fide* contract or agreement whatever.

When we undertake to prove that it is right, according to law, for any person (free from all incumbrances or lawful demands) to bestow his own property or services to any amount, and to whomsoever he sees fit, it seems like an undertaking to prove that two and two make four. The right to give alms and to make donations either in property or labor is guarantied by the laws and usages of all nations. Landed property may, under some governments be entailed, but even estates-tail are considered by us as inconsistent with the genius of a free republic; because the possessor of such estate is restrained in his disposal of it. Even in England, legal finesse is resorted to, to break the shackles which had been antiently imposed upon the right of giving away property as the proprietor of it pleases.

No one, we think, can seriously doubt of the legal right, which every man in this country possesses of giving away and receiving property according to the very order and manner practised by the Church.

Another inquiry is raised on the ground of Equity. Admitting it is consistent with the rules and maxims of law, will it comport with the pure principles of Justice and Equity?

Answer. In the first place, let us examine wherein there is, or may be a difference between Law & Equity. It may be supposed that the Law, that is, our written or statute laws, are defective by reason of that universality of expression which nothing but a closer-going principle of Equity can correct by reaching the minutest circumstance of every case. The written law cannot be made so explicit as to include in the strictest terms of expression or fair implication all that is necessary, in order to bring to justice the artful and designing, by tracing them through all their dark and crooked windings, and those subtle schemes which they invent to entrap and defraud the less artful or more honest.

A court is therefore instituted for the relief of such sufferers, and this is called a court of Equity. In this court the judge may decide according to evidence and the common or written law. Where there is no statute that will bear him through; he may select and apply the principles of Common Law to the case in hand; & where he can find none to suit, he takes such as are most analogous and, according to his own scrutinizing judgment, raises up a new principle, or correcting law, by which he decides the case. This important subject requires a serious attention, in order to discover its just merits.

The Church would be supposed to be so deeply interested that a righteous decision could not, from that quarter, be expected; and of course, the withdrawing member, all his near relations, every other member who has left the Society, and every one who intends to leave it, are, by reason of their self interest in the adjudication, incapable of being impartial. We have no alternative now left, but to look to those who are the least liable to be influenced by interest, and who at the same time, are the most capable of understanding such matters. This will lead us directly to the Court of Equity, by reason of its superior advantages in obtaining the evidence of the facts, as well as its extensive powers in gathering the opinions and judgments, the laws and usages of the wisest and best men who have lived for many ages past.

And what would or could such a tribunal do in the present case? In this court, as well as all others, the decision must be given according to law and evidence.

Here the Covenant is the evidence of the fact, that the withdrawing member did voluntarily give his property and services for the uses therein specified; and also that he therein promised never to make any charge or demand for the same.

Here the fact is clear and indisputable; and the court

acknowledged rule of judgment. Now to understand this last appeal fairly, the question is, What rule of judgment is to be considered as most binding on the moral sense or conscience of a Christian? It will be answered, the revealed will of God as recorded in the scriptures of the Old and New Testaments. Then, "to the law and to the testimony; if they speak not according to this word, it is because there is no light in them." (Isa. 8, 20.)

We will first mention the positive requirements under the law. One tenth of all their increase was to be consecrated: in addition to this every first born male of man and beast. These, with other positive requirements under the law, plainly show that God holds a claim to property, and to persons too, for his special service. And were those large donations ever credited to the donor, with any view to a recovery?

But beyond positive requirements, there was an abundance of free-will offerings which were encouraged and highly approbated. All vows and promises to dedicate to the service of God, either property or person, were approved and confirmed. And however they might, under the influence of the selfish principle, afterwards change their minds, they were never permitted to fail in the fulfilment of their sacred voluntary engagements. "If a man vow a vow unto the Lord—he shall not profane his word, he shall do according to all that proceedeth out of his mouth." (Num. 30, 2.) No provision here for any change of mind.

Now what think ye, did Christ come to destroy the law, or to fulfil it?—Did he teach his disciples to be more selfish, more penurious, or more tenacious of their property than had been customary? Just the reverse.

The law by levying on a part, for the purpose of supporting union, only served as a school master to bring us to Christ, whose doctrine required an entire devotion of all that a man had, and his own consecrated life into the bargain. Let him that readeth understand.— "Whosoever he be of you that forsaketh not all that he hath, he cannot be my disciple." (Luke 14, 33.)

Hence the example of the poor widow was so highly commended, in putting into the treasury all that she had

and that the Common Law secures to all sane persons, who are not under duress or constraint, the power of making such donations of property or of services, as they have a just claim to. The Court of Equity, therefore, as well as that of rigid justice must and will decree that the donation was lawfully and rightfully made; & that the Covenant by which the gift was secured is lawful and good, and that any act or decree that would disannul or make it void, would be wrong and altogether immoral in its tendency, as it would, in effect, destroy all covenants or agreements, deeds, and obligations, in short that the whole foundation of social compact or intercourse between man and man would be swept away, & that breach of premise would no more be wrong.

Thus we see by the authority that is deemed the most wise and the most pure on earth, it is established, that it would not be right but wrong, for the withdrawing member to break his vow, or make any demand for such consecrated service or property. Whence it follows of course, that whatever he can rightfully receive must be given to him, according to the provisions of the Covenant, as a charity.

Most clearly then, any one losing his right of membership, by renouncing his faith and his former obligations of obedience, has no better claims to privileges, property or support, than those who never were members. But those and those only who acknowledge and obey the faith and doctrines of the gospel, and conform to the rules and orders thereof, are held in relation as members.

But in the next place, admitting that no law of man can reach the case, may it not be expected that for conscience toward God, remuneration will be made? We answer, All that conscience has to do in the matter is, to require the judgment to be honestly exercised to decide the case according to the best light, rule, or law which it may be in possession of.—And as we have already seen what the decision would be of a conscientious judge, when guided by the best rules or laws among men; so there can be no propriety in appealing to conscience, unless she be allowed to have access to some

C

even her whole living, altho it was but about a farthing. For the gospel requires a full surrender, to God from those who profess it, and any one under the profession of obedience to the Gospel, in full Church relation, attempting to hold back a part of his property or services for self, may remember Ananias and Sapphira.—— And how could any one stand on any better ground who had solemnly and freely given up all, should he ever afterwards attempt to take back a part or the whole of what he had freely devoted? For any thing further on this point, we refer to the ever memorable facts recorded in the acts of the Apostles, where it is said, "The multitude of them that believed were of one heart, and of one soul; neither said any of them that aught of the things which he possessed, was his own; but they had all things common." (Acts, 4, 32.)

Is there any evidence that aught of this property was ever reclaimed, or that there ever was an order of court either in heaven or on earth to repeal those gifts, and subject the Church to debt or damage for the same?

The result of this inquiry, then, is obvious; that conscience has no other concern in the matter, except to acquiesce in the principles of right established by all the aforesaid authorities, and decide accordingly.

Some, for mere evasion, have brought up the golden rule of doing to others as we would they should do to us, and as they would fondly apply it, we think a greater absurdity could not be invented. We are willing this rule should be applied to us in any rational point of view; it is that by which we square our conduct in all our transactions with mankind, but should we follow the ignisfatuous light of a self-interested apostate and his advocate, where would it lead us?

But what do we do to others, that we would not that they should do to us?—We covet no man's silver or gold, or property of any description, of course we wish them not to covet ours,—we demand nothing from any man to which we have not a lawful right? and why should we not repel an unlawful demand upon us? and as we punctually keep and fulfil our contracts, so we wish others to do.—And tho we vow to our own hurt, we change not, (see Psa. 15, 4.) And could we wish others to act differently? But should we at any time, recant a fair bargain, and attempt by law to force our opponent into a compliance with our covetous wishes, we would that the court should brand such a suit with infamy;—Then let such be the result of all illegal claims against the church, and all differences of opinion on this interesting subject will be fairly and impartially settled

Here we think the argument might close, but one final objection, on account of serious minds, we shall consider; viz. that this final dedication is carrying the matter too far, further than the general sense of mankind will approbate, consequently renders the institution unpopular: whereas by some little alterations in the church covenant, permitting the withdrawing member to take back his property, and allowing him something for his labor, the institution might be more extensive and useful.

Answer. Had we been set to contrive the plan, no doubt we should have adopted such views; but all we have had to do in the matter has been, to receive it as it has been originally constructed by a higher authority.

But to obviate what Dr. Clelland of Kentucky terms its "*odious unpopularity*,"[*] we would remark, that every degree of the work of God that has ever been introduced among mankind, has been *odiously unpopular* in its commencement. By consulting Dr. Lardner's quotations from the book of Celsus it will appear how popular Christ himself was, in the early days of his ministry. But so it is that every step in the travel of the church

[*] *See Unitarianism Unmasked p.* 161.
It is worthy of remark that Dr. Clelland could find nothing more manly, with which to meet "Dunlavy's Manifesto" *than the unpopularity of the cause which it espoused. I think his cheek must redden, when he comes to reflect that, in the gospel glass he is viewed as near of kin, to Celsus, that ancient and very popular abuser of the character of our blessed Savior.* "*Thou unbelieving Thomas, please to read Dr. Lardner,* as above quoted, *and I think you will despair of riding into the temple of fame, on the* "*odious unpopularity*" *of modern Believers! Ed.*

towards her consummate glory, has been under an increasing cross.—The circumcised Jew was *odiously unpopular* to the whole gentile world, and Christians, as long as they maintained the circumcision of Christ, supported no better character in the esteem of a licentious world, from which the conclusion is evident, as it respects the finishing work of God in this latter day;— that it must be by a full cross that the church can possibly arrive at her consummate glory.

No one is compelled to bear such a cross, but when the time is fully come for Zion to arise and put on her beautiful garments, and a people are prepared to take up such a cross, is it consistent that God should suspend his purposes and procrastinate his work, because it is likely to be *unpopular*, and but a few ready to approbate it?

The *unpopular* few who chuse to advance to the hight of Zion, cannot interrupt any that chuse to tarry on the plain of mere partnership and self-interest, but as an apology for our holding fast what we have received, let us for a moment take a view of a society constituted on the *popular* plan.

Here all are equally prepared and invited to flock together, the multitude must include whole families, old and young, rich and poor, weak and strong with their several interests, talents and faculties. All go to work that are able and willing, and all derive their support from the joint stock, each has his property appraised, and his money and property, of course, going on interest.

Who, now, is to register those several sums, and calculate the annual interest, and keep book for a fair reckoning of loss or gain? Who is sufficiently versed in arithmetic, to calculate the value of the days works performed by this popular assembly, and make the proper deductions for boarding, washing, lodging, clothing, doctoring and other necessary expenses; all which must be done if each is to retain his personal interest, and a legal and just settlement is to be made. And without such regular accounts, what sworn jury could *legally guess* what the annual labor of an individual was worth, or how much ought to be deducted for necessary and contingent expenses. But we leave it to those who have attempted the experiment, or may wish to establish a community on such a plan, to make the calculation. We have but one object in view, and that is to fulfil, in the most unequivocal manner, "all that the prophets have spoken" concerning the church of God in the latter day. And thus after examining the subject on every side, it evidently appears, that the unity, purity and perpetuity of the Church can never be gained and supported, except upon those very principles upon which this institution is founded.

And here we shall close this subject with a few passing remarks on this pure principle of selfdenial, and impartial regard to the welfare of others,—a principle which induces its subject to give, hoping for no remuneration in this world, and freely to exchange the selfish & contracted pleasures of time, for the more sublime and exalted enjoyments for which man was created.

That such a principle does exist, and that wherever seen, it ought to claim universal approbation, a few actions, under peculiar circumstances seem to prove.— A spirit of benevolence in doing good to the poor, in a man's hazarding his own life to save the life of his fellow creature, in his suffering toil and danger for his country's sake without pecuniary reward; how are these things admired! how are such characters eulogized!— what an immortal renown accompanies their names!

Of this truth we have a signal instance in George Washington. And what, pray, did he do, which constrains all to honor him? Why, he perseveringly endured privations and hardships; was faithful, zealous and enterprizing in the cause in which he was engaged; refused pecuniary reward for his arduous services; and lastly (and this crowned all) he did not do what so many successful chiefs have done: he did not usurp the sovereign power when it was within his grasp: but resigned up his commission and retired in peace. What is it then, that calls forth unbounded and universal esteem, but a measure of self denial, so conspicuous through the different parts of his public life as well as his private walks?

Here we see that God has a witness in every man's breast, which is compelled to honor and approve of the principle of self denial. How little soever they may exercise it, they are ready to testify its heavenly origin.

How must mankind feel when they come to see and know that the Church, as to its principles, is founded wholly on the doctrine of selfdenial, and that it is built up, entirely, by the practice thereof.—If one man should be induced, through friendship, to give up his own life to save the life of his friend, and do it deliberately, his fame would be sounded far and near, especially if that friend should be some person of note. But how must the world be confounded when all come to know that every simple cross-bearing Believer (and that there are hundreds of such) is constantly in a work which requires him to lay down his earthly, sensual, and devilish life, in sure and certain hope of gaining a better, according to the promise of Christ, (John 12, 25) " He that loveth his life, shall lose it; and he that hateth his life in this world, shall keep it to life eternal."

SUPPLEMENTARY

It will be remembered, that the order of the Church was introduced, entered into, and supported at New-Lebanon, for a number of years before any thing like a written covenant was thought of, and it was only for the security of their just and natural rights, on account of those who were envious without; and for the more perfect information of all whom it might afterwards concern, that this legal instrument was resorted to. It was at first, and still is, intentionally, the confirmation of a bona fide *contract, and as such, has been admitted as testimony, in courts of law, where the evidence of facts has required it.*

It has always stood open for amendments if necessary, & has passed through sundry Editions.—In some Societies it has been occasionally revised for the purpose of holding forth its principles in the clearest possible light; and as an authentic form of its entire obligations has been anxiously sought by many, the following is offered to the reader as a true & proper sample of the general principles, as unitedly understood and formally subscribed, by way of Revision and confirmation of the original ground, on which the institution of Church order commenced.

FORM OF A REVISAL & RATIFICATION
OF
THE CHURCH COVENANT;
OR
The principles, and terms of Church-membership, in the United Society of Believers, called Shakers.

WHEREAS in the year of our Lord one thousand, eight hundred and   a Society was formed in this place, now called   in the county of   and State of   denominated Believers in Christ's second Appearing, and commonly known by the name of Shakers: which Society, according to the rights and liberties of consience guarantied by the constitution & laws of the land, adopted the faith and principles, rules manners, and customs held forth by the gospel of Christ in his first and second appearing; and having for the term of   years, proved the said faith and principles, in what is called the Junior order; and being well satisfied therewith, in order to lay a permanent foundation for the comfortable support of all who then chose or afterward might chuse to devote themselves to that manner of life, independent of the personal claims of private individuals; it was agreed by the said Society, jointly, to constitute and establish a consecrated interest to which no individual could hold any personal or private claim; the said interest to be secured in the hands of Trustees, for the equal use and benefit of all such as might associate together in church-relation : Accordingly a written covenanant, bearing date   was entered into by the members of said society; by virtue of which covenant, a Ministry has been duly established, Trustees appointed, lands and tenements purchased and improved, the subscribing members of the Church duly organized as a body, and the various rules and regulations pertaining to church-order introduced and put into practice : And whereas, for the more perfect adjustment of the affairs of the Church thus constituted and established, it is deemed proper to renew the said covenant in its primitive and true sense and meaning, and to ratify all its fundamental articles; Therefore,

We, whose names are hereunto subscribed do, hereby recognize, as fundamental articles of the aforesaid covenant, the following particulars.

I. As heretofore, so now, we jointly and severally acknowledge our faith in the foundation laid at New Lebanon, in the State of New York; and still believe, as heretofore, that the doctrines, rules, manners and customs, heretofore taught, and hitherto supported, are to be regarded as the ground work of church-order and spiritual relation; that according to those wholesome rules, the ministerial gift is first in authority, in every community of Believers, by which all subordinate agents or officers in care, whether spiritual or temporal are to be chosen and appointed.

II. That as heretofore, so it continues to be fit and proper, for certain individuals to be intrusted with the care & management of the temporalities of the Church, as deacons or Trustees,—That it is the duty of such trustees to take the immediate charge and oversight of all & singular the property, estate & interest, devoted and given up to the joint use and benefit of the Church, with all gifts, grants, and donations that may, at any time, be given or devoted for the benefit of the Church, or for the relief of the poor, or any such charitable use or purpose. And as heretofore, so now & henceforth, the said interest cannot be considered as subject to partnership claims, nor any partition of the capital, seeing it is expressly declared by said covenant, that the said interest shall be and remain forever, inviolably, under the care and oversight of the deaconship, in a continual line of succession; and, that all the transactions of the Deacons, in the management and disposal of said property, shall be for the mutual benefit of the Church jointly, & to no personal or private end or purpose whatever.

III. As heretofore, so now, all who are received as members of the Church are to be of lawful age to act for themselves; and such as have property, and are free from debt, are allowed to bring in and devote all such property as they hold and have an indisputable right to, as their lawful interest. But no account is kept, nor reckoning made of what the individual has bestowed; nor is it right there should, seeing he is an equal partaker of the gifts of others; as all and every individual belonging to said church shall enjoy equal rights and privileges, in the use of all things provided for their common support, as every one has need, without any difference made on account of what any one brought in.

And as heretofore, so it remains, that all the members are in duty bound to support and maintain the said interest according to their several abilities, and let the labor or service be what it may, it never was, nor is the manner, custom, or rule of the Church to make or keep any account of the personal property, the labor or service of any member, as matter of debt, damage or blame, or for the members of the Church to bargain or deal with each other upon any principle of personal or separate interest whatever; Therefore,

IV. As heretofore expressed, so it remains, that there is no foundation in law or Equity, upon which any member of the Church whatever, can ever bring any charge of debt, damage or blame, before any civil tribunal, against the Church, or any member thereof, or any other person whatever, on account of any thing devoted as aforesaid.

And moreover, as we have heretofore agreed, and expressly declared that we, personally, hold no legal claims to the said consecrated property, and that our services are mutually and gratuitously bestowed, for the benefit and support of each other;—and as the titles of real estate so consecrated, are legally settled and duly adjusted, in the order of the trusteeship, and, moreover, as the proceeds and benefits of our mutual labors, are placed in a due line of order, for the benefit and comfort of the community: In order to ratify, confirm, settle, and secure the object intended by all concerned; *We Do*, by these presents, and in conformity to the said original covenant, solemnly agree with each other, for ourselves, our heirs, executors, and administrators, never hereafter, to bring debt or demand against the Deacons of the Church, nor against their successors, nor against any member of the Church or community, on account of any of our services or property thus devoted to the use and benefit of the said community. *In witness &c.*

A few Reflections on the foregoing Covenant.

To show that the temporal interest held by the United Society, never was intended, nor can be appropriated to the wealth or personal aggrandizement of a few, or only a part of said Society; we submit the following summary of facts, to present the reader with a kind of synopsis of the general plan. And, first; —we most pointedly assert that we have adopted the present mode of life, from the most conscientious motives and principles,—that our temporal interest is held in conformity to the order of the Primitive Church of Christ;—that this dedication does not end with the lives of those who thus dedicate it; but descends in perpetuity to a regular heirship, who can never apply it to any other purposes than those stipulated in our *constitution or covenant*.—That the said instrument is equally binding upon all the members in these respects. The Ministry and Elders can exercise no control over said property, otherwise, than to direct the disposal of it according to the covenant, personally, they hold nothing more than unofficial members.—The Trustees only hold, and manage the temporalities in trust; and are as responsible for their conduct as any other member. But these temporal arrangements, however economical, fall far short of unfolding the inward principle by which the concern is managed. The most important consideration which leads us to be so explicit on these points, is to regulate the public mind, by offering every thing on the subject that would tend to inform or edify.—And we should think that a very moderate portion of discernment might enable any unbiassed mind to discover, that such a devoted, self-denying life as is led by the devotees of this institution, has but very few charms for abstracted, worldly minded, wealth accumulating mortals; for those who are truly greatest among us, are the least of all, and servants of all. The truth is, our kingdom is not from hence, and we only consider the things of this life of secondary importance,—and think it duty to "use the things of this world as not abusing them, for the fashion of this world passeth away."

To show the light in which our church-covenant has been viewed in courts of justice, in these days of generous freedom, we shall close with a brief extract from a speech of the Honorable John Brethett of Kentucky.

"And is it matter of objection against any man, that his motives are so pure and disinterested, that he desires to be released from earthly thraldom, that he may fix all his thoughts and affections on his God? after they have signed the covenant, they are relieved from earthly care.

"Much has been urged against Shakerism, much has been said against their covenant. But, sir, I repeat it, *that* individual who is prepared to sign the Church covenant stands in an enviable situation;—his situation is, indeed, an enviable one; who, devoted to God, is prepared to say of his property:—Here it is, little or much, take it and leave me unmolested to commune with my God.—I deed, I dedicate myself to what? rot to a fanatical tenet: Oh no! to a subject far beyond—to the worship of Almighty God, the great Creator and Governor of the universe! Under the influence of his love, I give my all;—Only let me worship according to my faith, and in a manner I believe acceptable to my God!

"Now what is there objectionable in all this? I say again, the world cannot produce a parallel to the situation which such a man exhibits. Resigned to the will of heaven, free from all the feelings of earthly desire;—and pursuing, quietly, the peaceful tenor of his way."

"Let us hear the conclusion of the whole matter:—Fear God and keep his commandments for this is the whole of man. [all besides (says Dr. Gill) is beast]—

For God will bring every work into judgment, with every secret thing, whether *it be* good, or evil."

THE PREACHER.

Edited by RICHARD M'NAMER and DAVID SPINING, Watervliet, June 30, 1832.

AN
IMPROVED EDITION
OF
THE CHURCH COVENANT,
OR
CONSTITUTION
OF
THE UNITED SOCIETIES,

CALLED SHAKERS.

Collated from the several copies which have been duly executed in the several Societies, respectively; and officially sanctioned by the several Ministries, for the purposes therein contained.

DAYTON (OHIO)
1833.

United States of America, to wit:

BE IT REMEMBERED, That in the month of September, in the year of our Lord 1829, it was proposed and recommended, by the Ministry and Elders of the Church at New-Lebanon, in the county of Columbia and state of New-York, to all the several branches of the Church under their care, to renew the Church-Covenant in such a manner as to embrace all the improvements and amendments, from time to time made and approved, and eventually, to establish one explicit Constitution, containing one uniform statement of our principles of association, adapted to the general circumstances of each Society:— That a draft of the said New-Covenant was then made, at New-Lebanon aforesaid, and the same circulated to all the several branches of the Church in the union, subject to any amendments or improvements that might be considered necessary and proper for the mutual satisfaction of all: That the said New-Covenant was read, duly examined, and with a few amendments, has been legally executed and subscribed by all, in every branch of the Church, who are deemed church-members in good standing. And whereas, in pursuance of the object proposed, it has been agreed to collate and combine all the several copies of said covenant, so executed, in such a manner as to embrace in one explicit copy, the sum and substance of the whole: And whereas the said explicit copy has been so made, and exhibited to the full understanding and free acceptance of all concerned; Therefore, in order to the ratification and final confirmation of the same; We the undersigned, composing the Ministry in the several societies throughout the union, having superintended the aforesaid transactions, in our several lots of care, and being fully satisfied that the said last-mentioned copy or form of the said general covenant, as hereinafter contained, is correct and without fraud or misrepresentation of any kind; do, by these presents, and by virtue of the authority constitutionally reposed in us, sanction, confirm and ratify the same, for all the intents and purposes therein specified.

In testimony whereof we have hereunto set our hands and affixed our Common Seal, &c. &c.

CONTENTS

ARTICLE I. *Of the Gospel Ministry*

SECTION	PAGE
I Their Origin, Call, and Institution.	37
II. Their Order and office.	38
III. Perpetuity of, and manner of filling that office.	ib
IV. Of the Ministerial office, in the several Societies.	ib.
V. Powers and duties of the Ministry.	39

ARTICLE II. *Institution of the Church.*

I. The Object and Design of Church-relation.	ib.
II. Who are not admissible to Church-membership.	40
III. Preparation for entering into Church-relation.	ib.
IV. Admission of New Members.	41
V. Concerning Youth and Children.	ib.

ARTICLE III. *Of the Trusteeship*

I. Appointment, Qualifications and Powers of Trustees.	ib.
II. Duties of the Trustees.	42
III. Trustees to be responsible to the Ministry and Elders.	ib.
IV. Account Books, and Books of Record, to be kept.	43
V. Trustees to execute a Declaration of Trust.	ib.
VI. Vacancies, in certain cases, how supplied.	44

ARTICLE IV. *Of the Eldership.*

I. Choice and appointment of Elders.	ib.
II. Duties of the Elders.	45

ARTICLE V. *Of Family-Deacons and Deaconesses*

I. Their Quaifications and appointment.	ib.
II. Their Duties and Obligations.	ib.

ARTICLE VI. *Of Church-Members.*

I. Benefits and privileges of members in Church-relation.	46
III. Obligations of the Members.	ib.
III. Duties of the Members.	47
IV. No special claims, in case of removals.	ib.

ARTICLE VII. *Dedication and Release.*

I. Dedication of persons, services and property.	ib.
II. Declaration and Release of private claim, & Confirmation.	48

AN IMPROVED EDITION
OF
THE CHURCH COVENANT.

WE the people of the UNITED SOCIETIES, known by the name of SHAKERS, and residing in different parts of the UNITED STATES, having sufficiently tested the principles rules, and regulations on which we are founded as a religious community, in order to confirm and increase our general union in the same, secure our equal rights and privileges, and convey to posterity a clear understanding of the nature and design of the gospel institution, *do make ordain,* and *declare* the following *Articles of Agreement,* as a Summary of the principles, rules and orders established throughout the community, to be kept and maintained as a *General Covenant,* or *Constitution,* which shall stand as a lawful testimony of our religious association, before all men, and in all cases of question and law, relating to the possession and improvement of our consecrated interest and estate, until the same be altered or amended by general agreement, and in union with the leading authorities of the institution.

ARTICLE I.

Sec. 1. *WE solemnly declare to each other, and to all whom it may concern,* that we have received and do hereby acknowledge, as the foundation of our faith, order and government, the testimony of the gospel of Christ, in his first and second appearing; and we do hereby solemnly agree to support and maintain the same, as ministered by the founders of this Society, and kept and conveyed through a regular order of ministration down to the present day: and altho we are variously associated, as to the local situations of our respective communities, yet we are known and distinguished as a peculiar people, and consider and acknowledge ourselves as members of *one general community,* possessing one faith, and subject to the administration of one united and uniform government, which has been regularly supported from the first foundation pillars of the institution, and which continues to operate, for the support, protection and strength of every part of said community.

Sec. 2. *We further acknowledge and declare,* That for the purpose of promoting and maintaining union, order and harmony throughout the various branches of the community, the primary authority, of the Institution has been, and is duly settled in the Ministry at New-Lebanon, in the county of Columbia and state of New York, there to remain as the *general* center of union to all who are held in gospel relation and communion. This Ministry consists of four persons, two of each sex.

Moreover, That the great local distance of the Societies in the western states, from the general center, requires a center of union in that quarter; and as the first opening of the gospel, and the establishment of church-order in the west, was at Union Village in the state of Ohio, by a regular emanation from the general center of union; it is proper that the Society at Union Village be the *central society,* and the *center of union* for all the branches of the Church in the western states.

Sec. 3. *We further acknowledge and declare,* That the primary authority aforesaid, has been, and is to be perpetuated as follows, to wit; That the first in the Ministry possess the right, to chuse and appoint their successors, who, being selected, and sufficiently instructed, grow up into a fitness to fill the place, with general approbation.[*] But in case that no such appointments be previously made, then the right to direct and authorize such appointments and other necessary regulations, devolves upon the surviving members of the Ministry, in council with the Elders of the Church and others, as the nature of the case, in their judgment, may require.

Sec. 4. *We further acknowledge and declare, covenant and agree,* That the ministerial office and authority in any Society of our faith, which has emanated, or may emanate from the center of union aforesaid, is, and shall be acknowledged, owned and respected, as vested with the spiritual authority of such Society, in all matters pertaining to the said ministerial office. And in case of

---

[*] Such appointments are not arbitrary,—not influenced by the choice of the individual, nor by a majority of votes among the members, but by a Spirit of union between the head and members, which excludes all selfishness and partyism. See Test. p. 475.

the decease, removal, or releasement of any individual of said Ministry, in any such Society, his or her lot & place shall be filled by agreement of the surviving Ministers in council with the Elders and others, as the nature of the case may require, together with the knowledge and approbation of the Ministry at New Lebanon aforesaid, to which they are responsible.

Sec. 5. *We further acknowledge and declare,* That the Ministry being appointed and established as aforesaid, are vested with the primary authority of the Church and its various branches; hence it becomes their special duty to guide and superintend the spiritual concerns of the Society, as a body of people under their care and government; and in connexion with the Elders, in their respective families or departments, who shall act in union with them, to give and establish such orders, rules, and regulations, as may be found necessary for the government and protection of the Church and Society within the limits of their jurisdiction:— and also to counsel, advise, and judge, in all matters of importance whether spiritual or temporal. And the said Ministry are also invested with authority, in connexion with the Elders as aforesaid, to nominate, and appoint to office, ministers, elders, deacons and trustees, and to assign offices of care and trust to such brethren and sisters as they the said Ministry and Elders shall judge to be best qualified for the several offices to which they may be appointed.

And we hereby covenant and agree, That such nominations and appointments being made, and officially communicated to those concerned, and receiving the general approbation of the Church, or of the families concerned, shall, thenceforth, be confirmed and supported, until altered or revoked by the authority aforesaid.

ARTICLE II.

Sec. 1. *We further acknowledge and declare,* That the great object, purpose, and design of our uniting together as a Church or body of people in social and religious compact, is, faithfully and honestly, to occupy and improve our various gifts and talents, both of a spiritual and temporal nature, for the service of God, for the honor of the gospel, and for the mutual protection, support, comfort and happiness of each other, as brethren and sisters in the gospel, and for such other pious and charitable purposes as the gospel may require.

Sec. 2. As the *unity, purity* and *stability* of the Church essentially depend on the character and qualifications of its members; and as it is a matter of importance, that it should not be incumbered with unqualified persons;— *Therefore, we agree,* That no member of any company or association in business or civil concern; no copartner in trade: no person under any legal involvement or obligation of service; no slave nor slave-holder; no insane person; no profane person, nor any person who lives in the wilful violation of any of the known and acknowledged principles of moral rectitude, shall be deemed qualified for admission into the covenant-relation and communion of the Church.

Sec. 3. In order that Believers may be prepared for entering into the sacred privilege of church-relation, it is of primary importance, that sufficient opportunity and privilege be afforded, under the ministry of the gospel, for them to acquire suitable instruction in the genuine principles of righteousness and true holiness; and also, that they should prove their faith by their practical obedience to the precepts of the gospel, according to their instructions. It is also indispensably necessary for them to receive the *uniting spirit of Christ,* and become so far of one heart and one mind, that they be willing to sacrifice all other relations for this sacred ONE. Another essential step is, to settle all just and equitable claims of creditors and filial heirs; so that whatever property they possess, it may be justly their own. When this is done, and they feel themselves sufficiently prepared to make a deliberate and final choice, to devote themselves, wholly, to the service of God, without reserve, and it shall be deemed proper, by the leading authority of the Church, after examination and due consideration to allow them to associate together in the capacity of a Church, or a branch thereof, in gospel order, they may then consecrate themselves & all that they possess to the service of God forever, and confirm the same by signing and sealing a written covenant predicated upon the principles herein contained, and by fulfilling, on their part, all its obligations.

Sec. 4. As the door must be kept open for the admission of new members into the Church, when duly prepared, it is agreed that each and every person who shall at any time after the date and execution of the church-covenant in any branch of the community, be admitted into the Church, as a member thereof, shall, previously, have a fair opportunity to obtain a full, clear, and explicit understanding of the object and design of the church-covenant, and of the obligations it enjoins on the members. For this purpose, he or she shall, in the presence of two of the Deacons or acting Trustees of the Church, read said covenant, or hear the same distinctly read; so as to be able, freely, to acknowledge his or her full approbation and acceptance thereof, in all its parts. Then he, she, or they, as the case may be, shall be at liberty to sign the same, and having signed and sealed it, shall, thenceforth, be entitled to all the privileges of other members; and shall also be subject to all the obligations of the original signers; and the signature or signatures thus added, shall be certified by the said deacons or trustees, together with the date thereof.

Sec. 5. Youth and children, being minors, cannot be received as members of the Church; yet it is agreed that they may be received under the immediate care and government of the Church, at the desire or consent of such person or persons as have a lawful right to such minors together with their own desire or consent: but no minor under the care of the Church, can be employed, therein, for wages of any kind.

ARTICLE III.

Sec. 1. It has been found necessary, in the established order of the society, in its various branches, that superintending deacons or agents should be appointed, and authorized to act as Trustees of the temporalities of the Church. They must be recommended by their honesty and integrity, their fidelity in trust, and their capacity for the transaction of business, of which qualifications the Ministry and Elders are to be the judges. These trustees are generally known among us, by the title of Office-deacons, of which there are usually two of each sex; and being appointed by the authority aforesaid, and supported by the general approbation of the Church, they are vested with power to take the charge and oversight of all the property, estate, and interest, dedicated, devoted, consecrated and given up for the benefit of the Church; to hold, in trust, the fee of all lands belonging to the Church; together with all gifts, grants and donations which have been, or may, hereafter, be dedicated, devoted, consecrated and given up as aforesaid: and the said property, estate, interest, gifts, grants and donations shall constitute the *consecrated and united interest* of the Church, and shall be held in trust by the said deacons, as acting Trustees in their official capacity, and by their successors in said office and trust forever.

Sec. 2. It is and shall be the duty of the said deacons or acting trustees to improve, use and appropriate the said united interest for the benefit of the Church, in all its departments, and for such other religious and charitable purposes as the gospel may require, and also to make all just and equitable defense, in law, for the protection and security of the consecrated and united interest, rights and privileges of the Church and Society, jointly and severally, as an associated community, as far as circumstances and the nature of the case may require. *Provided nevertheless*, that all the transactions of the said Trustees, in the management, protection, defense and disposal of the aforesaid interest, shall be for the benefit and privilege, and in behalf of the Church or of the Society as aforesaid, and not for any private interest, object or purpose whatever·

Sec. 3. It shall also be the duty of the said Trustees, to give information to the Ministry & Elders, concerning the general state of the temporal concerns of the Church and Society committed to their charge; and also to report to said authority all losses sustained in the united interest thereof, which shall come under their cognizance:— and no disposal of any of the real estate of the Church, nor any important contract shall be considered as valid, without the knowledge and approbation of the authority aforesaid, to whom the said Deacons or Trustees are and shall, at all times, be held responsible in all their transactions.

Sec. 4. It shall be the duty of the said office-deacons to keep, or cause to be kept, regular Books of account, in which shall be entered the debit and credit accounts of all mercantile operations and business transactions between the Church and others—all receits and expenditures, bonds, notes and bills of account, and all other matters that concern the united interest of the Church.— Also, a Book or Books of Record, in which shall be recorded a true and correct copy of this covenant; also all appointments, removals and changes in office, of Ministers, Elders, Deacons and Trustees; all admissions, removals, departure and decease of members; together with all other matters and transactions of a public nature which are necessary to be recorded for the benefit of the Church, and for the preservation and security of the documents, papers and written instruments pertaining to the united interest and concerns of the Church committed to their charge. And the said records shall be annually inspected by the leading authorities of the Church; and they, together with the Trustees, shall be the official auditors of the same; and the signature of any one or more of said auditors, with the date of inspection and approval, shall be deemed sufficient authority for the correctness of the facts and matters so recorded.

Sec. 5. For the better security of the consecrated and united interest of the Church to the proper uses and purposes stipulated in this Covenant, it shall be the duty of the Trustee or Trustees, who may be vested with the lawful title or claim to the real estate of the Church, to make and execute a Declaration of Trust, in due form of law, embracing all and singular the lands, tenements, and hereditaments, with every matter of interest pertaining to the Church, which, at the time being, may be vested in him or them, or that may in future come under his or their official charge, during his or their said trusteeship: and the said declaration shall state expressly, that such Trustee or Trustees hold such lands, tenements, hereditaments, and all the personal property of every description, belonging to the Church, in trust, for the uses and purposes expressed *in*, and subject to the rules, conditions and regulations prescribed *by* the covenant or constitution of the said Church, or any amendments thereto which shall hereafter be adopted by the general approbation of the Church, and in conformity to the primitive faith and acknowledged principles of the Society: and the said Declaration shall be in writing, duly executed under the hand and seal of such trustee or trustees, and shall be recorded in the book of records provided for in the preceding section.

Sec. 6. *We further covenant and agree,* That in case it should, at any time happen, that the office of trustee should become vacant, by the death or defection of all the Trustees in whom may be vested the fee of the lands or real estate belonging to said Church or Society; then and in that case, a successor or successors shall be appointed by the constitutional authority recognized in this covenant, according to the rules and regulations prescribed by the same: and the said appointment being duly recorded in the Book of Records provided for in this article, shall be deemed, and is hereby declared to vest in such successor or successors all the right, interest and authority of his or their predecessors, in respect to all such lands, property or estate belonging to the Church or Society aforesaid.

ARTICLE IV.

Sec. 1. THE united interests and objects of Believers established in gospel-order, require that Elders should be chosen and appointed for the spiritual protection of families, who are to take the lead in their several departments, in the care and government of the concerns of the Church, and of the several families pertaining to the Society. Their number and order should correspond with that of the Ministry. They are required to be persons of good understanding, of approved faithfulness and integrity, and gifted in spiritual administration.— They must be selected and appointed by the Ministry, who are to judge of their qualifications.

Sec. 2. As faithful watchmen upon the walls of Zion,

it becomes the duty of the Elders to watch over their respective families; to instruct the members in their respective duties, to counsel, encourage, admonish, exhort and reprove, as occasion may require;—to lead the worship; to be examples to the members, in their obedience to the principles and orders of the gospel, and to see that the orders, rules and regulations pertaining to their respective families or departments be properly kept.

ARTICLE V,

Sec. 1. The office of family Deacons and Deaconesses has long been established in the Church, and is essentially necessary for the care, management and direction of the domestic concerns of each family, order or branch of the Church. They are required to be persons of correct and well-grounded faith in the established principles of the gospel; faithful in duty; closely united to their Elders, and of sufficient capacity for business. Of these qualifications the Ministry and Elders, by whom they are chosen and appointed, must be the judges.— Their number in each family is generally two of each sex, but may be more or less according to the size of the family and the extent of their various duties.

Sec. 2. The Deacons and Deaconesses of families are intrusted with the care and oversight of the domestic concerns of their respective families. It is their duty to make proper arrangements in business; to maintain good order; to watch over, counsel and direct the members in their various occupations, as occasion may require; to make application to the office-deacons for whatever supplies are needed in the several departments of the family, to maintain union, harmony and good understanding with the said office-deacons, and to report to their Elders the state of matters which fall under their cognizance and observation. But their power is restricted to the domestic concerns of their several families or departments and does not extend to any immediate or direct intercourse with those without the bounds of the Church:— They have no immediate concern with trade and commerce;—It is not their business to buy and sell, nor in any way dispose of the property under their care, except with the union and approbation of the Trustees.

ARTICLE VI.

THE united interest of the Church having been formed by the free-will-offerings and pious donations of the members respectively, for the objects and purposes already stated, it cannot be considered either as a joint-tenancy, or a tenancy in common, but a consecrated *whole*, designed for and devoted to the gospel forever, agreeable to the established principles of the Church; Therefore, it shall be possessed and enjoyed by the Church, in their united capacity, as a sacred and covenant right: that is to say, all and every member thereof, while standing in gospel-union, and maintaining this covenant, shall enjoy equal rights, benefits and privileges in the use of all things pertaining to the Church, according to their several needs and circumstances; and no difference shall be made on account of what any one has contributed and devoted, or may hereafter contribute and devote to the benefit of the institution.

Sec. 2. It is, nevertheless, provided, stipulated, and agreed, that in case any one, having signed this Covenant, should, afterwards, forfeit his or her claim to membership, by renouncing the principles of the Society, or by wilfully and obstinately violating the rules thereof, (of which the Ministry and Elders of the Church shall be the proper and constitutional judges) then and in that case, his or her claim to all the aforesaid benefits, privileges and enjoyments, shall be equally forfeited.

Sec. 3. As subordination and obedience are the life and soul of every well regulated community; so our strength and protection, our happiness and prosperity in our capacity of church-members, must depend on our faithful obedience to the rules and orders of the Church and to the instruction, counsel and advice of its leaders. Therefore:—*We do hereby covenant and agree*, that we will receive and acknowledge as our Elders, in the gospel those members of the church who are or shall be chosen and appointed, for the time being, to that office and calling, by the authority aforesaid; and also, that we will, as faithful brethren and sisters in Christ, conform and subject to the known and established principles of our community, and to the counsel and direction of the

Elders who shall act in union as aforesaid; and also, to all the orders, rules and regulations which now are, or which may be given and established in the Church, according to the principles and by the authority aforesaid.

Sec. 4. The faithful improvement of our time and talents in doing good, is a duty which God requires of mankind as rational and accountable beings, and more especially as members of the Church of Christ: therefore, it is, and will be, required of all and every member of this Institution, unitedly and individually, to occupy and improve their time and talents to support and maintain the interest of the same—to promote the objects of this Covenant, and discharge their duty to God, according to their several abilities and callings, as members in union with one common lead; so that the various gifts and talents of *all*, may be improved for the mutual benefit of *each* and all concerned.

Sec 5. As we esteem the mutual possession and enjoyment of the consecrated interest and privileges of the Church, fully adequate to any contribution made by any individual; so we consider that no ground of action can lie, either in law or equiy, for a recovery of any matter or thing devoted as aforesaid. *And we further agree, That, in case any member or members shall remove from one family, Society, or branch of the Church to another, his, her or their signature or signatures to the church-covenant shall forever bar all claims, which are incompatible with the true intent and meaning of this covenant, in such manner as if such removal had not taken place; yet all who shall so remove, with the approbation of their elders, shall be entitled to all the benefits and privileges of the order in which they shall be placed, as long as they shall conform to the rules and regulations of the same.*

ARTICLE VII.

Sec. 1. According to the faith of the gospel which we have received, and agreeably to the uniform practice of the Church of Christ, from its first establishment in this Society, WE COVENANT and AGREE to dedicate devote, consecrate and give up, *and by this Covenant we do, solemnly and conscientiously,* dedicate, devote, consecrate and give up ourselves and our services, together with all our temporal interest, to the service of God and the support and benefit of his Church, and to such other pious and charitable purposes as the gospel may require, to be under the care and direction of the proper constituted authorities of the Church as aforesaid, according to the true intent and meaning of this covenant, and the rules of the Church heretofore known and practised.

Sec. 2. WHEREAS, in pursuance of the requirement of the gospel, and in the full exercise of our faith, reason and understanding, we have freely and voluntarily sacrificed all self-interest, and have devoted our persons, services, and property, as aforesaid, to the pious and benevolent purposes of the gospel: *Therefore, We do,* hereby, solomnly and conscientiously, unitedly and individually, for ourselves our heirs and assigns, release and quitclaim to the deacons or acting trustees of the church, for the purposes aforesaid, ALL our private personal right, title, interest, claim and demand, of, in and to the estate, interest, property and appurtenances, so consecrated, devoted and given up: And we hereby, jointly and severally, promise and declare, in the presence of God and before witnesses, that we will never hereafter, neither directly nor indirectly, under any circumstances whatever, contrary to the stipulations of this Covenant, make nor require any account of any interest, property, labor or service, nor any division thereof, which is, has been, or may be devoted by us or any of us, to the uses & purposes aforesaid; nor bring any charge of debt or damage, nor hold any claim nor demand whatever, against the said Deacons or Trustees, nor against the Church or Society, nor against any member thereof, on account of any property or service given, rendered, devoted or consecrated to the aforesaid sacred and charitable purposes.—Hereby also ratifying and confirming every act and deed which we or any of us have acted or done, agreeably to the true spirit intent and meaning of this covenant. *In confirmation of all the aforesaid statements, covenants, promises and Articles of agreement, we have hereunto set our hands and affixed our seals on and after the* 29th *day of December in the year of our Lord* 1829.

THE COVENANT,

OR

CONSTITUTION OF THE CHURCH,

AT UNION-VILLAGE, (OHIO)

WE the brethren and sisters, of the United Society of Believers (called Shakers) residing in the county of Warren and State of Ohio, being connected together as a religious and social community, distinguished by the name and title of "The Church of the United Society at Union Village:"—which, for many years has been established, and in successful operation under the charge and protection of the Ministrry and Eldership thereof feeling the importance, not only of renewing and confirming our spiritual covenant with God and each other, but also of renewing and improving our social compact and amending the written form thereof; DO make, ordain and declare the following Articles of agreement, as a summary of the principles, rules & regulations established in the Church of our said United Society, which are to be kept and maintained by us, both in our collective and individual capacities, as a Covenant or Constitution which shall stand as a lawful testimony of our religious association, before all men, and in all cases of question and law relating to the possession and improvement of our consecrated interest, property and estate.

ARTICLE I.

Sec. 1. *WE solemnly declare to each other, and to all whom it may concern*, that we have received and do hereby acknowledge, as the foundation of our faith, order and government, the testimony of the gospel of Christ, in his first and second appearing; and we do hereby solemnly agree to support and maintain the faith and principles, the rules and manners pertaining to the said gospel, as ministered by the first founders of this Society, and kept and conveyed through a regular order of ministration down to the present day: and altho we are variously associated, as to the local situations of our respective communities, yet we are known and distinguished as a peculiar people, and consider and acknowledge ourselves as members of *one general community*, possessing one faith, and subject to the spiritual administration of one united parental and ministerial gift, which has been regularly supported from the first foundation pillars of the institution, and which continues to operate, for the support, protection and strength of every part of said community.

Sec. 2. *We further acknowledge and declare,* That for the purpose of promoting and maintaining union, order and harmony throughout the various branches of this community, the primary gift of parental authority has been settled in the first established Ministry at New-Lebanon, in the county of Columbia and state of New York, there to rest and remain as the *general* center of union to all who are held in gospel relation and communion. This Ministry consists of four persons, two of each sex.

Sec. 3. *We further acknowledge and declare,—* That the aforesaid primary gift of parental authority has been, and is perpetuated as follows, Namely— That the first in that office and calling possess the right by the sanction of Divine authority, given through the first founders of this Society to prescribe or direct any regulation or appointment which they may judge most proper and necessary, respecting the Ministry, or any other important matter which may concern the welfare of the Church subsequent to their decease.

But in case no such regulation or appointment be so prescribed or directed, then the right to direct and anthorize such regulations and appointments devolves upon the surviving members of the Ministry, in council with the Elders of the Church and others, as the nature of the case, in their judgment, may require.

Sec. 4. *We further acknowledge and declare, covenant and agree,* That the ministerial office and authority in any Society or community of our faith, which has emanated, or may emanate, in a regular line of order, from the center of union aforesaid, is, and shall be acknowledged owned and respected, as vested with the spiritual authority of such Society, in all matters pertaining to the said ministerial office. And in case of the decease, removal, or releasement of any individual of said Ministry, in any such Society, his or her lot and place shall be filled by agreement of the surviving Ministers in council with the Elders and others, as the nature of the case may require, together with the knowledge and approbation of the primary gift of authority at New Lebanon aforesaid, to which they are responsible.

Sec. 5. *We further acknowledge and declare,* That the

Ministry being appointed and established as aforesaid, are vested with the primary authority of the Church and its various branches; hence it becomes their special duty to guide and superintend the spiritual concerns of the Society, as a body of people under their care and government; and in connexion with the Elders, in their respective families or departments, who shall act in union with them, to give and establish such orders, rules, and regulations, as may be found necessary for the government and protection of the Church and Society within the limits of their jurisdiction:— and also to counsel, advise, and judge, in all matters of importance whether spiritual or temporal. And the said Ministry are also invested with authority, in connexion with the Elders as aforesaid, to nominate, and appoint to office, ministers, elders, deacons and trustees, and to assign offices of care and trust to such brethren and sisters as they the said Ministry and Elders shall judge to be best qualified for the several offices to which they may be appointed.

And we hereby covenant and agree, That such nominations and appointments being made, and officially communicated to those concerned, and receiving the general approbation of the Church, or of the families concerned, shall, thenceforth, be confirmed and supported, until altered or revoked by the authority aforesaid.

ARTICLE II.

Sec. 1 *We further acknowledge and declare*, That the great object, purpose and design of our uniting together as a Church or body of people in social & religious compact, is, faithfully and honestly, to occupy and improve our various gifts and talents, both of a spiritual and temporal nature, for the service of God, for the honor of the gospel; and for the mutual protection, support, comfort and happiness of each other, as brethren and sisters in the gospel, and for such other pious and charitable purposes as the gospel may require.

Sec. 2. As the *unity, purity* and *stability* of the Church essentially depend on the character and qualifications of its members; and as it is a matter of importance, that it should not be incumbered with persons who are under any involvement or incapacity either natural or moral; *Therefore, we agree,* That no member of any company or association in business or civil concern; no copartner in trade: no person under any legal involvement or obligation of service; no slave or bond-servant; no insane person; no profane person, nor any person who lives in the wilful violation of any known principle of moral rectitude, shall be deemed qualified for admission into the covenant-relation and communion of the Church.

Sec. 3. In order that Believers may be prepared for entering into the sacred privilege of church-relation, it is of primary importance, that sufficient opportunity and privilege be afforded, under the ministry of the gospel, for them to acquire suitable instruction in the genuine principles of righteousness and true holiness; and also, that they should prove their faith by their practical obedience to the precepts of the gospel, according to their instructions. It is also indispensably necessary for them to receive the *uniting spirit of Christ*, and become so far of one heart and one mind, that they are willing to sacrifice all other relations for this sacred ONE. Another essential step is, to settle all just and equitable claims of creditors and heirs; so that whatever property they may possess, it shall be justly their own. When this is done, and they feel themselves sufficiently prepared to make a deliberate and final choice, to devote themselves, wholly, to the service of God, without reserve, and it shall be deemed proper, by the leading authority of the Church, after examination and due consideration, to allow them to associate together in the capacity of a Church, or a branch thereof, in gospel order, they may then consecrate themselves and all that they possess to the service of God forever, and confirm the same by signing and sealing a written covenant predicated upon the principles herein contained, and by fulfilling, on their part, all its obligations.

Sec. 4. As the door must be kept open for the admission of new members into the Church, when duly prepared, it is agreed that each and every person who shall at any time after the date and execution of the church-covenant in any branch of the community, be admitted into the Church, as a member thereof, shall, previously, have a fair opportunity to obtain a full, clear, and explicit understanding of the object and design of the church-covenant, and of the obligations it enjoins on the members. For this purpose, he or she shall, in the presence of two of the Deacons or acting Trustees of the Church, read[said covenant,]or hear the same distinctly read; so as to be able, freely, to acknowledge his or her full approbation and acceptance thereof, in all its parts. Then he, she, or they, as the case may be, shall be at liberty to sign the same, and having signed and sealed it, shall, thenceforth, be entitled to all the privileges of other members; and shall also be subject to all the obligations of the original signers; and the signature or signatures thus added, shall be certified by the said deacons or trustees, together with the date thereof.

Sec. 5. Youth and children, being minors, cannot be received as members of the Church; possessing a consecrated interest in a united capacity;yet it is agreed that they may be received under the immediate care and government of the Church, at the desire or consent of such person or persons as have a lawful right to such minors together with their own desire or consent: but no minor under the care of the Church, can be employed, therein, for wages of any kind.

ARTICLE III.

Sec. 1. It has been found necessary, in the esstablished order of the Society, in its various branches, that superintending deacons or agents should be appointed. and authorized to act as Trustees of the temporalities of the Church. They must be recommended by their honesty and integrity, their fidelity in trust, and their capacity for the transaction of business. of which qualifications the Ministry and Elders are to be the judges. These trustees are generally known among us, by the title of Office-deacons, of which there are usually two of each sex; and being appointed by the authority aforesaid, and supported by the general approbation of the Church, they are vested with power to take the charge and overight of all the property, estate, and interest, dedicated, devoted, consecrated and given up for the benefit of the Church; to hold, in trust, the fee of all lands belonging to the Church; together with all gifts, grants and donations which have been, or may, hereafter, be dedicated devoted, consecrated and given up as aforesaid: and the said property, estate, interest, gifts, grants and donations shall constitute the *consecrated and united interest* of the Church, and shall be held in trust by the said deacons, as acting Trustees in their official capacity, and by their succesors in said office and trust forever.

Sec. 2. It is and shall be the duty of the said deacons or acting trustees to improve, use and appropriate the said united interest for the benefit of the Church, in all its departments, and for such other religious and charitable purposes as the gospel may require, and the said Trustees, according to counsel may judge proper; and also to make all just & equitable defense, in law, for the protection and security of the consecrated and united interest, rights and privileges of the Church and Society, jointly and severally, as an associated community, as far as circumstances and the nature of the case may require. *Provided nevertheless*, that all the transactions of the said Trustees, in the management, protection, defense and disposal of the aforesaid interest, shall be for the benefit and privilege, and in behalf of the Church or of the Society as aforesaid, and not for any private interest, object or purpose whatever.

Sec. 3. It shall also be the duty of the said Trustees, to give information to the Ministry & Elders, concerning the general state of the temporal concerns of the Church and Society committed to their charge; and also to report to said authority all losses sustained in the united interest thereof which shall come under their cognizance;—and no disposal of any of the real estate of the Church, nor any important contract shall be considered as valid, wthout the knowledge and approbation of the authority aforesaid, to whom the said Deacons or Trustees are and shall, at all times, be held responsible in all their transactions.

Sec. 4. It shall be the duty of the said office-deacons to keep, or cause to be kept, regular Books of account, in which shall be entered the debit and credit accounts of all mercantile operations and business transactions between the Church and others—all receipts and expenditures, bonds, notes and bills of account, and all other matters that concern the united interest of the Church.— Also, a Book or Books of Record, in which shall be recorded a true and correct copy of this covenant; also all appointments, removals and changes in office, of Ministers, Elders, Deacons and Trustees; all admissions, removals, departure and decease of members; together with all other matters and transactions of a public nature which are necessary to be recorded for the benefit of the Church, and for the preservation and security of the documents, papers and written instruments pertaining to the united interest and concerns of the Church committed to their charge. And the said records shall be annually inspected by the leading authorities of the Church; and they, together with the Trustees, shall be the official auditors of the same; and the signature of any one or more of said auditors, with the date of inspection and approval, shall be deemed sufficient authority for the correctness of the facts and matters so recorded.

Sec. 5. For the better security of the consecrated and united interest of the Church to the proper uses and purposes stipulated in this Covenant, it shall be the duty of the Trustee or Trustees, who may be vested with the lawful title or claim to the real estate of the Church, to make and execute a Declaration of Trust, in due form of law, embracing all and singular the lands, tenements, and hereditaments, with every matter of interest pertaining to the Church, which, at the time being, may be vested in him or them, or that may in future come under his or their charge of office, during his or their said trusteeship. And the said Declaration so executed shall be recorded in the book of records provided for in the preceding section.

ARTICLE IV.

Sec. 1. THE united interests and objects of Believer established in gospel-order, require that Elders should be chosen and appointed for the spiritual protection of families, who are to take the lead in their several departments, in the care and government of the concerns of the

Church, and of the several families established in and pertaining to the Society. Their number & order should correspond with that of the Ministry. They are required to be persons of blameless character, of approved faithfulness and integrity, and gifted in wisdom and spiritual administration. They must be selected and appointed by the Ministry, who are to judge of their qualifications.

Sec. 2. As faithful watchmen upon the walls of Zion, it becomes the duty of the Elders to watch over their respective families; to instruct the members in their respective duties, to counsel, encourage, admonish, exhort and reprove, as occasion may require;—to lead the worhip; to be examples, to the members, of meekness, patience, and obedience to the principles and orders of the gospel, and to see that the orders, rules and regulations perainting to their respective families or departments are properly kept.

ARTICLE V,

Sec. 1. The office of family Deacons and Deaconesses has long been established in the Church, and is essentially necessary for the care, management and direction of the domestic concerns of each family, order or branch of the Church. They are required to be persons of correct and well-grounded faith in the established principles of the gospel; honest—upright—just—impartial and faithful in duty; closely united to their Elders, and of sufficient capacity for business. Of these qualifications the Ministry and Elders, by whom they are chosen and appointed, must be the judges.—Their number in each family is generally two of each sex, but may be more or less according to the size of the family and the extent of their various duties.

Sec. 2. The Deacons and Deaconesses of families are intrus ed with the care and oversight of the domestic concerns of their respective families. It is their duty to make proper arrangements in business; to maintain good order; to watch over, counsel and direct the members in their various occupations, as occasion may require; to make application to the office-deacons for whatever supplies are needed in the several departments of the family to maintain union, harmony and good understanding with the said office-deacons, and to report to their Elders the state of matters which fall under their cognizance and observation. But their power is restricted to the domestic concerns of their several families or departments and does not extend to any immediate or direct intercourse with those without the bounds of the Church—They have no immediate concern with trade and commerce;—It is not their business to buy and sell nor in any way dispose of the property under their care, except with the union and approbation of the Trustees.

ARTICLE VI.

THE united interest of the Church having been formed by the free-will-offerings and pious donations of the members respectively, for the objects and purposes already stated, it cannot be considered either as a joint-tenancy, or a tenancy in common, but a consecrated interest, designed for and devoted to the gospel forever, agreeable to the established principles of the Church; Therefore, it shall be possessed and enjoyed by the Church, in their united capacity, as a sacred and covenan-right: that is to say, all and every member thereof while standing in gospel-union, and maintaining this covenant, shall enjoy equal rights, benefits and privileges in the use of all things pertaining to the Church, according to their several needs and circumstances; and no difference shall be made on account of what any one has contributed and devoted, or may hereafter contribute and devote to the benefit of the institution.

Sec. 2. It is, nevertheless, provided, stipulated, and agreed, that in case any one, having signed this Covenant, should, afterwards, forfeit his or her claim to membership, by renouncing the principles of the Society, or by wilfully and obstinately violating the rules thereof, (of which the Ministry and Elders of the Church shall be the proper and constitutional judges) then and in that case, his or her claim to all the aforesaid benefits, privileges and enjoyments, shall be equally forfeited.

Sec. 3. As subordination and obedience are the life and soul of every well regulated community; so our strength and protection, our happiness and prosperity in our capacity of church-members, must depend on our faithful obedience to the rules and orders of the Church and to the instruction, counsel and advice of its leaders. Therefore: *We do hereby covenant and agree*, that we will receive and acknowledge as our Elders, in the gospel those members of the church who are or shall be chosen and appointed, for the time being, to that office & calling by and in the order and manner aforesaid; and also, that we will, as faithful brethren and sisters in Christ, conform and subject to the known and established principles of our community, and to the counsel and direction of the Elders who shall act in union as aforesaid; and also, to all the orders, rules and regulations which now are, or which may be given and established in the Church, according to the principles and by the authority aforesaid.

Sec. 4. The faithful improvement of our time and talents in doing good, is a duty which God requires of man as a rational and accountable being, and this duty is indispensible in the members of the Church of Christ: therefore, it is, and will be, required of all and every member of this Institution, unitedly & indiviually to occupy and improve their time and talents to support and maintain the interest of this Society, to promote the objects of this Covenant, and discharge their duty to God, according to their several abilities and callings, as members in union with one common lead; so that the various gifts and talents of *all*, may be improved for the mutual benefit of *each* and all concerned. *And we further agree, That, in case any member or members shall remove from one family, Society, or branch of the Church to another, his, her or their signature or signatures to the church-covenant shall forever bar all claims, which are incompatible with the true intent and meaning of this covenant, in such manner as if such removal had not taken place; yet all who shall so remove, with the approbation of their elders, shall be entitled to all the benefits and privileges of the order in which they shall be placed, as long as they shall conform to the rules and regulations of the same.*

ARTICLE VII.

Sec. 1. According to the faith of the gospel which we have received, and agreeably to the uniform practice of the Church of Christ, from its first establishment in this Society, WE COVENANT and AGREE to dedicate devote, consecrate and give up, *and by this Covenant we do, solemnly and conscientiously,* dedicate, devote, consecrate and give up ourselves and our services, together with all our temporal interest, to the service of God and the support and benefit of his Church, and to such other pious and charitable purposes as the gospel may require, to be under the care and direction of the Ministry, Elders, Deacons and Trustees that now are, or may be appointed and established in the Church, in the manner and by the authority aforesaid.

Sec. 2. WHEREAS, in pursuance of the requirement of the gospel, and in the full exercise of our faith, reason and understanding, we have freely and voluntarily sacrificed all self-interest, and have devoted our persons, services, and property, as aforesaid, to the pious and benevolent purposes of the gospel: *Therefore, We do,* hereby, solomnly and conscientiously, unitedly and individually, for ourselves our heirs and assigns, release and quitclaim to the deacons or acting trustees of the church, for the purposes aforesaid, ALL our private personal right, title, interest, claim and demand, of, in and to the estate, interest, property and appurtenances, so consecrated, devoted and given up: And we hereby, jointly and severally, promise and declare, in the presence of God and before witnesses, that we will never hereafter, neither directly nor indirectly, under any circumstances whatever, contrary to the stipulations of this Covenant, make nor require any account of any interest, property, labor or service, nor any division thereof, which is, has been, or may be devoted by us or any of us, to the uses & purposes aforesaid, nor bring any charge of debt or damage, nor hold any claim nor demand whatever, against the said Deacons or Trustees, nor against the Church or Society, nor against any member thereof, on account of any property or service given, rendered, devoted or consecrated to the aforesaid sacred and charitable pur poses.—*In confirmation of all the aforesaid statements, covenants, promises and Articles of agreement, we have hereunto subscribed our names and affixed our seals on and after the 31st day of December, Anno Domini* 1829.

THE ELDERSHIP

James Smith, Stephen Spining, Elizabeth Sharp, Rosalinda Watts, Eli Houston, William Sharp, Caty Boyd, Anna Brownfield, Daniel Sering, Abner Bedle, Anna Boyd' Charlotte Morrell, Th's Taylor, And'w C. Houston, Eliza Sharp, Caty Rubart, Joseph c. Worley, Jacob Holoway, Nanco Millikin, Jane Buchannan, Clark Valentine, Daniel Davis, Vincy M' Namer, Peggy Knox, John Gee jr,

TRUSTEES

Nathan Sharp, Lewis Valentine Polly Thomas, Betsy Dickson,

Thomas Hunt, Amos Valentihr, Betsy Wait, Susanna Liddil, William Davis, Sam'l Holoway, Joanna Woodruff, Betsy Patterson William Runyon, Daniel Miller, Esther Davis Rachel Duncan, Jesse Legier, Jenny Slater

Francis Bedle, Joseph Stout John Houston, John Dennis, John Carson, George Legier, Charles West, William Wilson, Joseph Johnson, Abner Bonnel, Belte. Draggoo, John Gee sr, John Miller, Elijah Davis, Sam'l A. Woodruff, Reuben Morris, Garner M' Namer, Loren Belcher, Alex. M' Keehen, Randolf West, Andrew Brown, Stephen Williams, Caleb Pegg, Lewis Wait, Garret Petirson, Cornelius Campbell, David B Cory, John Able, James Hodge, Wm More, Wm Bridge, Daniel Staggs, David Price, Chauncy Daniels, Joseph Francis, Jotham Slack, Henry Tann, James Easton, John Dennis jr. Henry Valentine, James M' Namer, S.W Hugh M' Namer, Moses Miller, Jacob Longstreth, Hiram Kimble. Richard M' Namer, Wm Redmon, Stephen C. Easton, Cephas Haloway, Jesse Duffey, Eliab Houston, Peter Boyd, S. Worthington, D. Redmon.

SISTERS—*Jenny M' Namer, Peggy Houston, Peggy Bigger, Nancy Rollins, Eunice Brown, Hannah Carson, Mary Spining, Eliz. Legier, Sarah Sering, Lydia Davis, Phebe Howard, Polly Patterson, Mary West, Hannah Holoway, Susanna Miller, Rebecca M' Neely, Rosanna Stout, Hanna Dennis, B. W. Caty Runyon, Sarah Hunt, Ruth Williams Mary Pegg, Polly Hardin, Sarah Caro, Anna Middleton Abigail Johnson, Betsy Murphy, Polly Rice, Prudence Redmon, Polly Belcher, Betsy Gandy, Frances Silence.*—Eunice Patterson, Rebecca Worley, Mary Kitchel, Betsy Dunlavy, Polly Clark, Eliz. Morris, Sally Baker, Polly Davis, Mary Graham, Eliz. Gallaghar, Rachel Dennis, Abigail Clark, Cynthia Hill, Betsy Evans, Sally Gee, Sally Slater, Phebe Able, Nancy Slater, Ruth Pegg, Lucy Anderson, Nancy Able. Polly Morris, Nancy Sering, Polly Stout, Loretta Hunt, Sally Brown,

THE CONSTITUTION,

OR

COVENANT OF THE CHURCH,

AT PLEASANT-HILL. (KENTUCKY)

WE the brethren and sisters, members of the United Society of Believers (called Shakers) residing at Pleasant-Hill, in the county of Mercer and State of Kentucky, having been, for many years, connected together as a religious and social community, by virtue of our distinguishing faith and mutual agreements; in order more fully to confirm our principles of government increase our union, improve our social compact, protect out equal rights & privileges, and secure to ourselves and our posterity in the gospel the blessings of peace and tranquility, Do mutually agree to adopt, and by these presents do adopt the following Articles of agreement, made, ordained and declared by the proper authorities of the Church of our said United Society in its senior departments, as a summary of the principles, rules and regulations originally established in said Church, and which we as members thereof, agree to keep and maintain, both in our collective and individual capacities, as a firm covenant which shall stand as a lawful testimony of the terms and conditions of our association, before all men, and in all cases of question and law relating to the possession and improvement of our consecrated interest, property and estate, until the same be altered or amended by general agreement, and in union with the leading authorities of the institution.

ARTICLE I.

Sec. 1. *WE solemnly declare to each other, and to all whom it may concern,* that we have received and do hereby acknowledge, as the foundation of our faith, order and government, the testimony of the gospel of Christ, in its first and second appearing; and we do hereby solemnly agree to support and maintain the faith and principles, the rules and manners pertaining to the said gospel, as ministered by the first founders of this Society, and kept and conveyed through a regular order of ministration down to the present day: and altho we are variously associated, as to the local situations of our respective communities, yet we are known and distinguished as a peculiar people, and consider and acknowledge ourselves as members of *one general community,* possessing one faith, and subject to the spiritual administration of one united parental and ministerial gift, which has been regularly supported from the first foundation pillars of the institution, and which continues to operate, for the support, protection and strength of every part of said community.

Sec. 2. *We further acknowledge and declare,* That for the purpose of promoting and maintaining union, order and harmony throughout the various branches of this community, the primary gift of parental authority has been settled in the first established Ministry at New-Lebanon, in the county of Columbia and state of New York, there to rest and remain as the *general* center of union to all who are held in gospel relation and communion. This Ministry consists of four persons, two of each sex.

Moreover, The Society at Union Village, in the county of Warren and State of Ohio, being first in their call and the obedience of faith, we do hereby agree to hold and respect the said Society as being first in order and constituted a leading and central society in these western States.

Sec. 3. *We further acknowledge and declare,—* That the aforesaid primary gift of parental authority has been, and is perpetuated as follows, Namely— That the first in that office and calling possess the right by the sanction of Divine authority, given through the first founders of this Society to prescribe or direct any regulation or appointment which they may judge most proper and necessary, respecting the Ministry, or any other important matter which may concern the welfare of the Church subsequent to their decease.

But in case no such regulation or appointment be so prescribed or directed, then the right to direct and anthorize such regulations and appointments devolves upon the surviving members of the Ministry, in council with the Elders of the Church and others, as the nature of the case, in their judgment, may require.

Sec. 4. *We further acknowledge and declare, covenant and agree,* That the ministerial office and authority in any Society or community of our faith, which has emanated, or may emanate, in a regular line of order, from the center of union aforesaid, is, and shall be acknowledged owned and respected, as vested with the spiritual authority of such Society, in all matters pertaining to the said ministerial office. And in case of the decease, removal, or releasement of any individual of said Ministry, in any such Society, his or her lot and place shall be filled by agreement of the surviving Ministers in council with the Elders and others, as the nature of the case may require, together with the knowledge and approbation of the primary gift of authority at New Lebanon aforesaid, to which they are responsible.

Sec. 5. *We further acknowledge and declare,* That the Ministry being appointed and established as aforesaid, are vested with the primary authority of the Church and its various branches; hence it becomes their special duty to guide and superintend the spiritual concerns of the Society, as a body of people under their care and government; and in connexion with the Elders, in their respective families or departments, who shall act in union with them, to give and establish such orders, rules, and regulations, as may be found necessary for the government and protection of the Church and Society within the limits of their jurisdiction:— and also to counsel, advise, and judge, in all matters of importance whether spiritual or temporal. And the said Ministry are also invested with authority, in connexion with the Elders as aforesaid, to nominate, and appoint to office, ministers, elders, deacons and trustees, and to assign offices of care and trust to such brethren and sisters as they the said Ministry and Elders shall judge to be best qualified for the several offices to which they may be appointed.

And we hereby covenant and agree, That such nominations and appointments being made, and officially communicated to those concerned, and receiving the general approbation of the Church, or of the families concerned, shall, thenceforth, be confirmed and supported, until altered or revoked by the authority aforesaid.

ARTICLE II.

Sec. 1 *We further acknowledge and declare,* That the great object, purpose and design of our uniting together as a Church or body of people in social & religious compact, is, faithfully and honestly, to occupy and improve our various gifts and talents, both of a spiritual and temporal nature, for the service of God, for the honor of the gospel, and for the mutual protection, support, comfort and happiness of each other, as brethren and sisters in the gospel, and for such other pious and charitable purposes as the gospel may require.

Sec. 2. As the *unity, purity* and *stability* of the Church essentially depend on the character and qualifications of its members; and as it is a matter of importance, that it should not be incumbered with persons who are under any involvement or incapacity either natural or moral ; *Therefore, we agree,* That no member of any company or association in business or civil concern; no copartner in trade: no person under any legal involvement or obligation of service; no slave or bond-servant; no insane person; no profane person, nor any person who lives in the wilful violation of any known principle of moral rectitude, shall be deemed qualified for admission into the covenant-relation and communion of the Church.

Sec. 3. In order that Believers may be prepared for entering into the sacred privilege of church-relation, it is of primary importance, that sufficient opportunity and privilege be afforded, under the ministry of the gospel, for them to acquire suitable instruction in the genuine principles of righteousness and true holiness; and also, that they should prove their faith by their practical obedience to the precepts of the gospel, according to their instructions. It is also indispensably necessary for them to receive the *uniting spirit of Christ*, and become so far of one heart and one mind, that they are willing to sacrifice all other relations for this sacred ONE. Another essential step is, to settle all just and equitable claims of creditors and heirs; so that whatever property they may possess, it shall be justly their own. When this is done, and they feel themselves sufficiently prepared to make a deliberate and final choice, to devote themselves, wholly, to the service of God, without reserve, and it shall be deemed proper, by the leading authority of the Church, after examination and due consideration to allow them to associate together in the capacity of a Church, or a branch thereof, in gospel order, they may then consecrate themselves and all that they possess to the service of God forever, and confirm the same by signing and sealing a written covenant predicated upon the principles herein contained, and by fulfilling, on their part, all its obligations.

Sec. 4. As the door must be kept open for the admission of new members into the Church, when duly prepared, it is agreed that each and every person who shall at any time after the date and execution of the church-covenant in any branch of the community, be admitted into the Church, as a member thereof, shall, previously, have a fair opportunity to obtain a full, clear, and explicit understanding of the object and design of the church-covenant, and of the obligations it enjoins on the members. For this purpose, he or she shall, in the presence of two of the Deacons or acting Trustees of the Church, read[said covenant,]or hear the same distinctly read; so as to be able, freely, to acknowledge his or her full approbation and acceptance thereof, in all its parts. Then he, she, or they, as the case may be, shall be at liberty to sign the same, and having signed and sealed it, shall, thenceforth, be entitled to all the privileges of other members; and shall also be subject to all the obligations of the original signers; and the signature or signatures thus added, shall be certified by the said deacons or trustees, together with the date thereof.

Sec. 5. Youth and children, being minors, cannot be received as members of the Church; possessing a consecrated interest in a united capacity; yet it is agreed that they may be received under the immediate care and government of the Church, at the desire or consent of such person or persons as have a lawful right to such minors together with their own desire or consent: but no minor under the care of the Church, can be employed, therein, for wages of any kind.

ARTICLE III.

Sec. 1. It has been found necessary, in the established order of the Society, in its various branches, that superintending deacons or agents should be appointed, and authorized to act as Trustees of the temporalities of the Church. They must be recommended by their honesty and integrity, their fidelity in trust, and their capacity for the transaction of business, of which qualifications the Ministry and Elders are to be the judges. These trustees are generally known among us, by the title of Office-deacons, of which there are usually two of each sex; and being appointed by the authority aforesaid, and supported by the general approbation of the Church, they are vested with power to take the charge and oversight of all the property, estate, and interest, dedicated, devoted, consecrated and given up for the benefit of the Church; to hold, in trust, the fee of all lands belonging to the Church; together with all gifts, grants and donations which have been, or may, hereafter, be dedicated devoted, consecrated and given up as aforesaid: and the said property, estate, interest, gifts, grants and donations shall constitute the *consecrated and united interest* of the Church, and shall be held in trust by the said deacons, as acting Trustees in their official capacity, and by their succesors in said office and trust forever.

Sec. 2. It is and shall be the duty of the said deacons or acting trustees to improve, use and appropriate the said united interest for the benefit of the Church, in all its departments, and for such other religious and charitable purposes as the gospel may require, and the said Trustees, according to counsel may judge proper; and also to make all just & equitable defense, in law, for the protection and security of the consecrated and united interest, rights and privileges of the Church and Society, jointly and severally, as an associated community. a far as circumstances and the nature of the case may require. *Provided nevertheless*, that all the transactions of the said Trustees, in the management, protection, defense and disposal of the aforesaid interest, shall be for the benefit and privilege, and in behalf of the Church or of the Society as aforesaid, and not for any private interest, object or purpose whatever·

Sec. 3. It shall also be the duty of the said Trustees, to give information to the Ministry & Elders, concerning the general state of the temporal concerns of the Church and Society committed to their charge; and also to report to said authority all losses sustained in the united interest thereof which shall come under their cognisance;—and no disposal of any of the real estate of the Church, nor any important contract shall be considered as valid, without the knowledge and approbation of the authority aforesaid, to whom the said Deacons or Trustees are and shall, at all times, be held responsible in all their transactions.

Sec. 4. It shall be the duty of the said office-deacons to keep, or cause to be kept, regular Books of account, in which shall be entered the debit and credit accounts of all mercantile operations and business transactions between the Church and others—all receits and expenditures, bonds, notes and bills of account, and all other matters that concern the united interest of the Church.— Also, a Book or Books of Record, in which shall be recorded a true and correct copy of this covenant; also all appointments, removals and changes in office, of Ministers, Elders, Deacons and Trustees; all admissions, removals, departure and decease of members; together with all other matters and transactions of a public nature which are necessary to be recorded for the benefit of the Church, and for the preservation and security of the documents, papers and written instruments pertaining to the united interest and concerns of the Church committed to their charge. And the said records shall be annually inspected by the leading authorities of the Church; and they, together with the Trustees, shall be the official auditors of the same; and the signature of any one or more of said auditors, with the date of inspection and approval, shall be deemed sufficient authority for the correctness of the facts and matters so recorded.

Sec. 5. For the better security of the consecrated and united interest of the Church to the proper uses and purposes stipulated in this Covenant, it shall be the duty of the Trustee or Trustees, who may be vested with the lawful title or claim to the real estate of the Church, to make and execute a Declaration of Trust, in due form of law, embracing all and singular the lands, tenements, and hereditaments, with every matter of interest pertaining to the Church, which, at the time being, may be vested in him or them, or that may in future come under his or their official charge, during his or their said trusteeship: and the said declaration shall state expressly that such Trustee or Trustees hold such lands, tenements, hereditaments, and all the personal property of every description, belonging to the Church, in trust, for the uses and purposes expressed *in*, and subject to the rules, conditions and regulations prescribed *by* the covenant or constitution of the said Church, or any amendments thereto which shall hereafter be adopted by the general approbation of the Church, and in conformity to the primitive faith and acknowledged principles of the Society: and the said Declaration shall be in writing, duly executed under the hand and seal of such trustee or trustees, and shall be recorded in the book of records provided for in the preceding section.

Sec. 6. *We further covenant and agree,* That in case it should, at any time happen, that the office of trustee should become vacant, by the death or defection of all the Trustees in whom may be vested the fee of the lands or real estate belonging to said Church or Society; then and in that case, a successor or successors shall be appointed by the constitutional authority recognized in this covenant, according to the rules and regulations prescribed by the same: and the said appointment being duly recorded in the Book of Records provided for in this article, shall be deemed, and is hereby declared to vest in such successor or successors all the right, interest and authority of his or their predecessors, in respect to all such lands, property or estate belonging to the Church or Society aforesaid.

ARTICLE IV.

Sec. 1. THE united interests and objects of Believers established in gospel-order, require that Elders should be chosen and appointed for the spiritual protection of families, who are to take the lead in their several departments, in the care and government of the concerns of the Church, and of the several families established in and pertaining to the Society. Their number & order should correspond with that of the Ministry. They are required to be persons of good understanding, of approved faithfulness and integrity, and gifted in spiritual administration. They must be selected and appointed by the Ministry, who are to judge of their qualifications.

Sec. 2. As faithful watchmen upon the walls of Zion, it becomes the duty of the Elders to watch over their respective families; to instruct the members in their respective duties, to counsel, encourage, admonish, exhort and reprove, as occasion may require;—to lead the worship; to be examples to the members, in their obedience to the principles and orders of the gospel, and to see that the orders, rules and regulations pertaining to their respective families or departments are properly kept.

ARTICLE V,

Sec. 1. The office of family Deacons and Deaconesses has long been established in the Church, and is essentially necessary for the care, management and direction of the domestic concerns of each family, order or branch of the Church. They are required to be persons of correct and well-grounded faith in the established principles of the gospel; faithful in duty; closely united to their Elders, and of sufficient capacity for business. Of these qualifications the Ministry and Elders, by whom they are chosen and appointed, must be the judges.— Their number in each family is generally two of each sex, but may be more or less according to the size of the family and the extent of their various duties.

Sec. 2. The Deacons and Deaconesses of families are intrusted with the care and oversight of the domestic concerns of their respective families. It is their duty to make proper arrangements in business; to maintain good order; to watch over, counsel and direct the members in their various occupations, as occasion may require; to make application to the office-deacons for whatever supplies are needed in the several departments of the family, to maintain union, harmony and good understanding with the said office-deacons, and to report to their Elders the state of matters which fall under their cognizance and observation. But their power is restricted to the domestic concerns of their several families or departments and does not extend to any immediate or direct intercourse with those without the bounds of the Church— They have no immediate concern with trade and commerce;—It is not their business to buy and sell nor in any way dispose of the property under their care, except with the union and approbation of the Trustees.

ARTICLE VI.

THE united interest of the Church having been formed by the free-will-offerings and pious donations of the members respectively, for the objects and purposes already stated, it cannot be considered either as a joint-tenancy, or a tenancy in common, but a consecrated interest, designed for and devoted to the gospel forever, agreeable to the established principles of the Church; Therefore, it shall be possessed and enjoyed by the Church, in their united capacity, as a sacred and covenant-right: that is, all and every member thereof while standing in gospel-union, and maintaining this covenant, shall enjoy equal rights, benefits and privileges in the use of all things pertaining to the Church, according to their several needs and circumstances; and no difference shall be made on account of what any one has contributed and devoted, or may hereafter contribute and devote to the benefit of the institution.

Sec. 2. It is, nevertheless, provided, stipulated, and agreed, that in case any one, having signed this Covenant, should, afterwards, forfeit his or her claim to membership, by renouncing the principles of the Society, or by wilfully and obstinately violating the rules thereof, (of which the Ministry and Elders of the Church shall be the proper and constitutional judges) then and in that case, his or her claim to all the aforesaid benefits, privileges and enjoyments, shall be equally forfeited.

Sec. 3. As subordination and obedience are the life and soul of every well regulated community; so our strength and protection, our happiness and prosperity in our capacity of church-members, must depend on our faithful obedience to the rules and orders of the Church and to the instruction, counsel and advice of its leaders. Therefore: *We do hereby covenant and agree,* that we will receive and acknowledge as our Elders, in the gospel those members of the church who are or shall be chosen and appointed, for the time being, to that office & calling by and in the order and manner aforesaid; and also, that we will, as faithful brethren and sisters in Christ, conform and subject to the known and established principles of our community, and to the counsel and direction of the Elders who shall act in union as aforesaid; and also, to all the orders, rules and regulations which now are, or which may be given and established in the Church, according to the principles and by the authority aforesaid.

Sec. 4. The faithful improvement of our time and talents in doing good, is a duty which God requires of man as a rational and accountable being, and this duty is indispensible in the members of the Church of Christ: therefore, it is, and will be, required of all and every member of this Institution, unitedly & indiviually to occupy and improve their time and talents to support and maintain the interest of this Society, to promote the objects of this Covenant, and discharge their duty to God, according to their several abilities and callings, as members in union with one common lead; so that the various gifts and talents of *all*, may be improved for the mutual benefit of *each* and all concerned. *And we further agree, That, in case any member or members shall remove from one family, Society, or branch of the Church to another, his, her or their signature or signatures to the church-covenant shall forever bar all claims, which are incompatible with the true intent and meaning of this covenant, in such manner as if such removal had not taken place; yet all who shall so remove, with the approbation of their elders, shall be entitled to all the benefits and privileges of the order in which they shall be placed, as long as they shall conform to the rules and regulations of the same.*

ARTICLE VII.

Sec. 1. According to the faith of the gospel which we have received, and agreeably to the uniform practice of the Church of Christ, from its first establishment in this Society, WE COVENANT and AGREE to dedicate devote, consecrate and give up, *and by this Covenant we do, solemnly and conscientiously,* dedicate, devote, consecrate and give up ourselves and our services, together with all our temporal interest, to the service of God and the support and benefit of his Church, and to such other pious and charitable purposes as the gospel may require, to be under the care and direction of the proper constituted authorities of the Church as aforesaid, according to the true intent and meaning of this covenant, and the rules of the Church heretofore known and practised.

Sec. 2. WHEREAS, in pursuance of the requirement of the gospel, and in the full exercise of our faith, reason and understanding, we have freely and voluntarily sacrificed all self-interest, and have devoted our persons, services, and property, as aforesaid, to the pious and benevolent purposes of the gospel: *Therefore, We do*, hereby, solemnly and conscientiously, unitedly and individually, for ourselves our heirs and assigns, release and quitclaim to the deacons or acting trustees of the church, for the purposes aforesaid, ALL our private personal right, title, interest, claim and demand, of, in and to the estate, interest, property and appurtenances, so consecrated, devoted and given up: And we hereby, jointly and severally, promise and declare, in the presence of God and before witnesses, that we will never hereafter, neither directly nor indirectly, under any circumstances whatever, contrary to the stipulations of this Covenant, make nor require any account of any interest, property, labor or service, nor any division thereof, which is, has been, or may be devoted by us or any of us, to the uses & purposes aforesaid, nor bring any charge of debt or damage, nor hold any claim nor demand whatever, against the said Deacons or Trustees, nor against the Church or Society, nor against any member thereof, on account of any property or service given, rendered, devoted or consecrated to the afor said sacred and charitable purposes.—*In confirmation of all the aforesaid statements, covenants, promises and Articles of agreement, we have hereunto subscribed our names and affixed our seals on and after the tenth day June, Anno Domini* 1830.

Elders—Edmund Bryant, Vincent Runyon, James Congleton, Th. Shain, Jacob Monfort, Ph. Linebach·—(*Tr*)-Ab-m Wilhite, John R. Bryant. (*De*)W. Runyon, Wm Verbrike, J. L. Ballance.)*Memb*) Joel Shields, Joseph Runyon, Jon. Vancleave, Stephen Manire,—Martin Runyon, Wm Shields, Lewis Wilhite, Ja. Coony Emley Runyon, Drury Woodrum, John Linebach &c.

CIRCULAR EPISTLE.

THE Ministry and Elders of the Church at New-Lebanon, to all who feel an interest in the prosperity of Zion, and claim a relation to the only gospel of salvation, in this day of Christ's second appearing.

DEARLY BELOVED GOSPEL-FRIENDS:—

Since it hath pleased God to call us by his grace and make us partakers of the blessed gospel of this latter-day, to be distinguished, in a sinful world, as a righteous and holy people, and to find our true relation to Christ and to each other, by our faithful obedience to the testimony of the cross.—And since, by the operations of Divine Wisdom, the treasures of the gospel have, in a special manner, been committed to our trust, we feel that we have a special duty to discharge at this time, which concerns us all, & to which we wish to call your particular attention. Feeling deeply interested in the increase of the gospel, we desire to impress on your minds a due consideration of certain matters, which, if rightly improved, will tend to increase our mutual strength and protection in the way of God, and promote a spirit of union and harmony among Believers.

In the first place, we feel to express our thanks to God and to his chosen agents, that through all the sufferings, afflictions and sore tribulations that have attended the second manifestation of Christ, the everlasting truth has been more and more displayed, so that our souls can rest with calm and unshaken confidence on that sure foundation, which, for more than half a century, has stood firm against all the storms of infidelity, vain phylosophy, antichristian influence, and the more dangerous intrigues of false-hearted brethren.

But notwithstanding so firm a foundation is laid, and so great a degree of prosperity has crowned the labors and sufferings of our pious predecessors and many of our cotemporaries, there is no provision made for us to lay aside our watchfulness, take our ease, and conclude that all is safe and beyond the reach of danger. Admitting (as perhaps we may) that our sacred profession has so far commended itself to the common protection of the civil authorities of our country, that but little persecution or opposition from without, is to be feared, have we as yet gained that degree of internal order that will secure us from the danger of losing the path of social and spiritual relation, as a consecrated people bound together by an inseparable bond of union? Is there not rather increasing cause for care and watchfulness, lest by any means some may be gradually and imperceptibly corrupted & drawn aside from the simplicity of that faith which has been planted and nourished by our first founders, and from those wholesome rules of order which we have been solemnly charged to keep and maintain?

Considering, *Dearly Beloved*, the extent to which the gospel has already spread: the many and various characters that are included in the profession of our faith & in the bonds of our fellowship: the boasted light and liberty that at this age greatly abound among mankind, and with which the sense & feeling of many who are admitted among us, are very full; and considering that it is very natural for such to desire to be teachers, and to mingle their treasures of worldly wisdom with the self-denying and mortifying doctrines of the cross, we would ask, —What security have we against all fear of degeneracy on the side of popularity, under a pretence of increasing light.

It has been sufficiently testified, and we are all fully convinced and satisfied, that the gospel has been introduced by that power and wisdom of God, that all the united wisdom of man cannot gainsay nor resist—and there still remain among us many living witnesses of the true increase of that wisdom, power & divine authority, which, step by step, has led the simple & honest-hearted into that pure and peaceful order, harmony and visible prosperity which has recommended the gospel to all souls that desire salvation. Is it not, therefore, of great importance, frequently, to call to mind the former days of gospel light, instruction and discipline, and retrace, in our memories the narrow path by which we have been led into the possession of this heavenly treasure? Believing as we do, that the present state of affairs, both in the civil and religious world, as well as among the several branches of our community, calls us unitedly & individually to a faithful examination of our state as a people, we feel it our duty to offer to all concerned a brief address on the subject, and call your mutual attention to what appears to be the special duty of the day.

And in the first place: Let it be remembered, that it was not by a convention of politicians–a general assembly of Divines, nor by the vote of a majority of Republicans, that the gospel of Christ was introduced among us. But when all human wisdom had failed, and a divided world of professing Christians were crying "Lo here! and lo there!" when awakened souls, groaning under the bondage of a corrupt nature, feeling and lamenting the baseness of human depravity, were crying to God for deliverance; then it was that one single mouth was opened, by one eternal spirit, to declare one only way of salvation and redemption, and one only door of entrance into one only kingdom of peace and happiness.

From the lips of our suffering and ever-blessed Mother that Testimony has gone forth, which will gather into one all things in Christ whether in heaven or on earth. Can it then be a matter of any doubt with us, whether the combined talents of proud mortals, or the spirit of *Eternal Truth* is to point out the path of our justification and dictate the plan of our association as a body The fallen race of man, from the remaining rays of original light and the improvements of human reason, may institute plans of government, and form laws for the regulation of civil society: but to regulate the work of God, as it respects the order of the gospel and the establishment of a spiritual kingdom on earth, no toleration can be given nor any room left for the clashing opinions or contrary senses of mortals to bear any sway.

Nominal Christians, by their own sagacity, may form their own Creeds and enact their own laws, and transform them into any shape that suits their own fancy: But when it is found, that in order to see the kingdom of God, there must of necessity be a new birth, How is that birth to be brought forth? Who can be born without a Mother? It is therefore a matter of the first importance with us, that we should ever realize our origin and descent, and acknowledge our relation to each other as children, not of the bond woman, but of the free; and according to our age and experience in the gospel, preserve the unity of the spirit, in the bond of peace.

During the ministration of our blessed first Mother, her gift of wisdom and kind maternal spirit, were all-sufficient to guide our infant faith, and lead our inexperienced feet in the paths of righteousness and peace.

Her word, whether in person or by her messengers or ministers, was a law to all her simple and honest-hearted children. And when her dispensation of parental instruction was finished, it was not left for her numerous offspring to settle by arbitrary appointment, or by the vote of a majority, which of them should be the greatest. The nursing-father stood ready in his place, to receive the weight and burden of the solemn charge committed to him. The labors and sufferings of Father James Whittaker, are never to be forgotten. Much is due to his faithfulness in superintending the concerns of the Society—in teaching, encouraging and strengthening the members, until, by experience and travel, they were prepared to constitute a spiritual body and bone come to its bone, and all the parts and organs of the living community commence their united operations.

We have all been well informed of the presiding gift which, according to prophecy, was vested in Father Joseph Meacham, for the gathering of Believers into church-order, It is also generally known, that this once unsightly, savage wilderness, now called New-Lebanon was chosen as the first consecrated ground for the establishment of the Church of this latter-day; and as yet, there remain many living witnesses of the special gifts and orders, which from time to time were given for the regulation of all matters both spiritual and temporal, particularly, for the establishment of a standing ministry, eldership, deaconship, trusteeship, and every lot of care and mutual help throughout the body. We may also call to mind the mutual sufferings and labors of our beloved Father Joseph and Mother Lucy, and all who were united with them, in gaining that order which was then considered and acknowledged as a pattern and example, to be followed by every association of Believers as far as the same work should extend.

It is also well known and ought forever to be remembered, that from this place, the law of Zion and the word of the Lord went forth to every place where the Testimony of Christ's second appearing is supported,— That is, ministers have been appointed and sent forth to open the testimony, and to instruct, lead and direct other souls as they themselves had been instructed, led, and directed; and they have always been considered responsible to the authority that sent them, for the faithful exercise of their office and trust. Through these means, our cords have been lengthened and our stakes strengthened, by an inward law of life & liberty which binds us together like the spreading branches of a fruitful vine. And our mutual faith and love are the only bonds of union that have been found necessary, so far as regards our relation to God and to each other as a separate and peculiar people. But with regard to our visible and external relation, as cognizable by the laws of civil society, and the use & disposal of our temporal interest, it has been and still is a matter of deep concern to us to support and maintain a consistent uniformity

In every place we are subject to the laws of the country in which we live. Those laws claim the same control over our temporal interest as over the interest of other citizens. Our interest must, therefore, be secured to the use intended, upon lawful grounds. Hence it becomes indispensibly necessary, that our temporal interest be secured in the hands of trustees, and that all our transactions, in thus arranging matters be legal and supportable in courts of justice and equity.

Laws are various in different states, and prejudices bear more or less sway every where; but in all countries mutual agreements, and written contracts supersede the interference of civil authorities. Mutual agreements in things lawful is, therefore, our only resource for the defense of our civil rights. Hence arises the necessity of a written covenant and a particular statement of the general principles of our church-order & form of government. But even this, when transformed into a legal instrument, without special care, is liable to be misunderstood & misconstrued, and to excite various sentiments even among good Believers and lead to such diversity of ideas and forms of expression, to suit the sense of the world, which may, if not carefully guarded against, finally, lead to unhappy divisions. and a kind of independence in the management of our temporal concerns.

Seeing, then, that we are, in reality, but one people, taught and governed by one spirit,—organized under one united ministerial gift, and constituted according to one order of government, we feel it our duty ro recommend to your consideration, the propriety and importance of having one explicit covenant adapted to the general circumstances of each Society, and containing one uniform statement of our principles of association, by which we may be able to assume one uniform ground of defense, in all cases that may occur under the authority of our respective States which boast the privileges and bear the name of United States-

With a view to accomplish this much-desired object, and leave at our decease a little legacy for our beloved youth and junior brethren and sisters, who are moving forward to fill our ranks as fast as they become vacant, we offer a form, for your consideration, which according to our experience and observation, will be found answerable to the work in this place, from the beginning, and which we deem neither dishonorable to the gospel of Christ, nor inconsistent with the laws of men.

It ought to be considered, that altho the senior institution at New-Lebanon, is a proper center for the general union, yet the great local distance of the Societies in the western States, from this place, requires a center of union in that quarter. And as the first opening of the gospel, and the first establishment of church-order commenced at Union Village in the State of Ohio, by a regular emanation, in the gift of God, from the general center of union, it is proper, in the order of God, that the Society at Union Village be the central Society & the leading gift in that place, the center of union for all the branches of the Church in the Western States.—The leading gift of that institution being regularly joined, and acknowledging the leading authority in the first center of union, will, of course, connect all the various branches to one center, like the branches of a flourishing vine to one root. This order ought to be stated in the written covenants of the various branches in the west.

To a uniformity in those external concerns, which so frequently bring Believers into contact with the world is very desirable, as it would contribute much to our strength and prosperity in the gospel, and to our conquest over the spirit of the world; yet we entertain no expectations that it can be obtained without our united exertions and faithful labors: and we fully believe, that as far as this proposition can obtain the united approbation of faithful Believers, so far it will effect one very important step toward this desirable object: Therefore let the exertions be made, in good faith, and the blessing of God will not fail to attend them.

There are some other matters which we feel it our duty to mention, and which must be gained before a general uniformity throughout the different societies can be attained. The first that we would notice, and which we consider a very important one, is that which relates to *party spirit & party politics*. This is a subject with which Believers ought never to intermeddle. Our faithful and beloved Father James, in his day, bore a strong and decided testimony against this spirit, and we sincerely desire that it may be wholly excluded from among Believers. No one can indulge himself in it, without feeling a growing and increasing bias of mind on one side or the other, which will imperceptably tend to mar his union and shut the gift of God out of his soul: the evils that will eventually follow, we need not mention, as every considerate Believer will readily perceive what they are, and the extent and magnitude of their influence.

2. Liberty of conscience.—As this is a sacred right, for the preservation of which, the witnesses of God in all ages have suffered more or less, and for which Believers have always been very strenuous in their own cases, we think it may not be amiss to caution them

against the abuse of it in themselves, under a delusive idea that they are justly contending for their liberty, when, in reality, they are striving for their own wills. (*This subject is abridged*)

3. There is another subject of importance which we feel it necessary to notice. It is that which respects the introduction of new improvements and inventions into the Society. * * * The work of God is a growing work, and the kingdom of Christ is an increasing kingdom: yet the work is of God and not of man, and the increase, with all its improvements, is to be brought forth in the gift of God, and according to the order of the gospel; not in the pursuit of our own ways, nor according to the imaginary ideas we may entertain of our own skill & talents. It is therefore of essential importance, to the maintenance of union and good order, that Believers, in all their labors for new improvements, whether in machinery, dress, manners or customs, be careful to proceed in union, and by no means to introduce new things into the Society, without the consent of the Ministry, and leading authority of the Church.

Finally, Beloved Brethren and Sisters, Farewell;—keep your faith unmarred, and walk in obedience to it;—keep yourselves unspotted from the world. "Avoid evil communications"—Cherish the bonds of your union as a dear and precious treasure, for it is your strength, and will necessarily lead you to more perfect obedience, and thereby protect you from the snares of the wicked one.

Accept this Address as a token of our kind love and remembrance, and our fervent prayers for your union, blessing, and prosperity in the gospel.

From the MINISTRY and ELDERS.

New-Lebanon, September 1, 1829.

"I do believe, as we are one people in the eye of the laws of the Union, as we have one standard of value, so we should have, for general purposes, one uniform circulating medium," (Speech of Senator Ewing)

THE CHURCH-COVENANT,

EXECUTED

At Union-Village, January 15th 1812.

THE STATE OF OHIO WARREN COUNTY.

WHEREAS we the subscribers, denominated by each other Believers in Christ, having received the testimony of the gospel through the ministration of the Church at New-Lebanon, in the township of Canaan, county of Columbia & state of New-York: and believing, according to the distinguishing faith of said Church, that Christ has actually made his appearance the second time without sin unto salvation, & has begun to establish his kingdom of righteousness and peace on earth, which is free to all people & will stand forever; and being made partakers of that light and power of God which has called and enabled us to take up a full and daily cross against the world, the flesh, & all evil in our knowledge, & to follow Christ in the regeneration, by which, we believe, God, according to his everlasting promise, will gather together in one all things in Christ, which are in heaven and upon earth, and having taken sufficient time & precaution to prove our faith, and being fully satisfied that it is the faith of the only true gospel into which we are called, and feeling it to be our duty and privilege, according to the holy Scriptures, the present call of God, and the civil and religious rights, secured to us in common with other citizens, to obey our faith, in all things, & to chuse that manner of life which we believe to be the most acceptable to God and most profitable to the spiritual and temporal good and welfare of ourselves and others;—And moreover, it being our faith, that the union and relation of the Church of God in one joint-interest, is a situation the most acceptable to God and productive of the greatest good of any state or situation attainable on earth; therefore in obedience to our own faith, we have dissolved every band and tie of the flesh or fallen nature of this lost world, and covenanted and agreed as brethren and sisters in the gospel, to gather together & unite in one body as a religious community; to be constituted, built up and established upon the principles and rules of the Church aforesaid. And as God, according to his promise, has begun to give his people one heart and one way, that they may serve him forever; we do therefore expressly agree to and with each other, that the order of God made known in his Church we will observe and keep, as delivered to us, with all and singular the rules, manners and customs of the Church, in relation to union, communion and fellowship; the rights, privileges and duties of the members, as also offices of trust and care, in the disposal and management of the joint-interest of the Church, according to the following articles of covenant.

I. We severally and jointly agree to gather together, and be constituted in the form and order of a Church, under the spiritual care of Elder David Darrow & Elderess Ruth Farrington, whom we acknowledge to be our beloved parents in the gospel, appointed by the gift of God to have the rule over us; and to watch for our souls and admonish us: Therefore, according to the rule and order of the gospel, it shall be our duty, at all times to reverence and respect them in their gift and calling, to be subject to them in the Lord, to follow their faith, and to esteem them very highly in love, for their works' sake.

II. That as it is fit and proper that certain individuals should be intrusted with the care of the temporal interest of the Church, as deacons or trustees; and as we believe that our beloved brethren Peter Pease, John Wallace and Nathan Sharp, are more particularly endowed with gifts and qualifications for that purpose, we do therefore call, appoint and ordain the said Peter Pease, John Wallace and Nathan Sharp, to the said office of deacons or trustees of the Church, mutually promising and covenanting to and with the aforesaid brethren, that they are duly invested with the said office of deacons or trustees, and empowered to exercise all the duties thereof, according to the rules and regulations of the Church heretofore known and practised, and which are herein after briefly stated.

III. All who are received as members of the Church,

are to be of lawful age to act for themselves, and to offer themselves freely and voluntarily, as a religious duty, and according to their own faith and desire, and such as have property, and are free from any just demand from those that are without, are allowed, according to their own faith, to bring in and devote, as a part of the joint-interest of the Church, all such property as they justly hold, and have an indisputable right to as their lawful interest; and the joint-interest of the Church thus formed and established by the free-will offerings of the members respectively, shall be possessed by the whole body jointly, as their natural and religious right; that is, all and every individual of or belonging to the Church shall enjoy equal rights and privileges in the use of all things pertaining to the Chh. according to their order and as every one has need, without any difference being made on account of what any one brought in; & it shall be the duty of all the members, to support and maintain the joint-interest of the Church, according to their several abilities, as members one of another, each in their order improving the manifold gifts of God for the good of the whole.

IV. That it shall be the duty of the deacons or trustees aforesaid, to take the immediate charge and oversight of all and singular the property, estate and interest dedicated, devoted and given up, as aforesaid, to the joint-interest of the Church—with all gifts, grants or donations, that may at any time be given or devoted for the benefit of the Church, or for the relief of the poor or any such charitable use or purpose; and the said joint-interest, estate, gifts, grants and donations shall be held by them, in the capacity of deacons or trustees, and shall be and remain forever, inviolably, under the care and oversight, and at the disposal of the deaconship of the Church, in a continual line of succession. And we do by these presents, covenant, promise and agree, that all the transactions of the deacons in the use and disposal of the joint-interest of the Church, shall be for the mutual benefit of the Church, and in behalf of the whole body, & to no personal or private end or purpose whatever. And when by death or any other means, any deacon or trustee shall cease to act in their office as aforesaid, then all & singular the power vested in, & duties incumbent upon them, shall devolve upon their successor who shall be appointed to fill their place in said office and trust; so that the individuals appointed to the office of deacons or trustees, of the church shall be vested with the power and authority of managing and disposing of the property and interest of the church, as aforesaid, and of making all just and lawful defense for the security and protection of the joint-interest and privileges of the church, and all the transactions of such members shall be valid, so long as they act in the official capacity of deacons or trustees in union with the body according to the tenor of this covenant, and no longer.

V. And further, we covenant and agree, that it shall be the duty of the trustees to keep, or cause to be kept in a *book* or *books*, provided for that purpose, a true copy of this covenant, together with all other records or matters of a public nature, that may be necessary for the information and satisfaction of all concerned, and for the security of the joint-interest of the church, committed to their care.

VI. *And moreover, as the whole end, design, and purpose of our thus uniting in church-relation is, to receive & diffuse the manifold gifts of God, to the mutual comfort & happiness of each other, as brethren and sisters in the gospel: and for the relief of the poor, the widow and the fatherless, and such as may be deemed real objects of charity:—Therefore, according to the faith, manner, rule, order and example of the Church, we do freely, and cordially, covenant, promise and agree together, each for ourselves, our heirs and assigns, that we shall never, hereafter, make any account of any property, labor or service devoted by us to the purposes aforesaid, or bring any charge of debt or damage, or hold any demand whatever against the church or community or any member thereof, on account of either property or service given, rendered, or consecrated to the aforesaid sacred and charitable uses. And in confirmation of all the aforesaid statements, covenants, promises & articles of agreement, we have hereunto subscribed our names, in presence of each other beginning on this fifteenth day of the first month, in the year of our Lord, one thousand eight hundred and twelve.*

PUBLIC NOTICE

THE Church (known by the name of Shakers) at Union Village and Watervliet, in the counties of Warren and Montgomery, state of Ohio, being constituted on the evangelical principles of a joint-interest, and accordingly, the property of the Church being secured by a firm covenant to pious and chritable uses and purposes, and committed to the lawful possession, care and management of certain individuals as deacons or trustees, who are solemnly bound to appropriate it to the use and benefit of the Church, the relief of the poor, the widow & fatherless and other objects of charity, but to no private or personal end or purpose whatever. And as contracts have, in some instances, been made by impostors, as agents of the Church, which contracts have been unauthorized by the Church and contrary to the foundation principles of the institution; Therefore, to prevent, in future, all imposition and fraud, either on the public or the Church, in relation to the said joint-interest, we present to the public the following extract from the church-covenant, which we are determined, punctually, to keep and maintain.

"As it is not our design, in supporting a joint-interest
'to lay up a treasure of this world's goods, but what is
'justly redeemed and consecrated to God, to use and im-
'prove to his honor and glory; therefore, it is our faith
'and agreement, never to bring into the joint-interest of
'the Church, by purchase or otherwise, any property
'which is not redeemed and free from all claim of debt
'or demand: and in all the transactions of the deacons or
'trustees, we mean that this rule be strictly observed,—
'never to bind themselves by any obligation or promise,
'that would be considered as bringing the joint-interest
'into debt. And should any person, in the name of a dea-
'con or trustee, or under any pretence whatever contract
'any debt on the pretended credit of the joint-interest of
'the Church, we shall not consider ourselves bound to
'answer it, but the individual shall be considered as out
'of union with us and personally accountable for his con-
'tracts. And furthermore, as it is our faith not to bring debt or blame on the Church for any of our transactions

and as we personally hold no legal claim to any part of 'the consecrated property of the Church; therefore, no 'deacon or trustee hath any right or authority to use the 'joint-interest in paying any debt or damage, or answer-'ing any demand that may come against any of us, as 'individuals, (otherwise than as a deed of charity.)"

Note. The above Article is not to be understood as laying any embarrassment in the way of crediting such members of the Society as hold personal property, and have never come into the order and relation of the Cäh. in supporting a joint-interest; but as the public cannot certainly distinguish between members of the Society in general, and members of the Church, or between the regular deacons of the Church and impostors, therefore we give this public notice, that in point of credit or trust there is no foundation for any distinction to be made; and the public are hereby forewarned from trusting any person or persons whatever, under our name or profession, beyond the evidence which they may give of their personal honesty and ability to fulfil their engagements; as we are determined that cash or property in hand shall be the only authority, legal power or credit, with which our orderly deacons shall ever be furnished, to make any purchase in behalf of the Church as a joint-Community

Signed in behalf of the Church, By us the Trustees, Deacons, & Elders of the Church—

	PETER PEASE,	NATHAN SHARP,
	DANIEL BOYD,	SAM'L HOLLAWAY,
	SAM'L ROLLINS,	WILLIAM RUNYON,
	ASHBEL KITCHELL,	FRANCIS BEDLE.
December	ELI HOUSTON,	JOSEPH STOUT,
28th 1818.	DAVID SPINING,	THOMAS TAYLOR,
	JA'S PATTERSON,	LEWIS VALENTINE.

N, B. The Church-covenant was renewed, July 14, '8'8 and this article added, in consequence of the apostasy and villainy of J. W. This Public Notice was directed by Father David,—drafted and witnessed by the subscriber, who still has the original in his possession, of which the foregoing is a true copy. ELEAZAR WRIGHT, C. S.

Watervliet, Feb. 20th 1834.

THE CHURCH-COVENANT,

EXECUTED

At Pleasant-Hill June 2nd, 1814.

THE STATE OF KENTUCKY *Mercer County.*

WHEREAS we the subscribers, denominated by each other Believers (implying such as believe in the present Testimony of Christ's second appearing) having received the gospel through the medium and ministration of the general Church, in the eastern states, whose center of union is the particular Church at New-Lebanon, in the township of Canaan, county of Columbia and state of New-York; from which place the messengers of the gospel were sent to us; and believing, according to the distinguishing faith of said Church, that Christ has actually made his appearance the second time without sin unto salvation, and has begun to establish his kingdom of righteousness & peace on earth, which is free to all people and will stand forever; and being made partakers of that light and power of God, by which we are enabled to take up a full and daily cross against the world, the flesh, & all evil in our knowledge, and to follow Christ in the regeneration, by which, we believe, God, according to his everlasting promise, will gather together in one all things in Christ, which are in heaven and upon earth, and having taken sufficient time and precaution to prove our faith, and being fully persuaded that this faith into which we are called, is the faith of the only true gospel, and believing it to be our duty and privilege, according to the holy Scriptures, the present call of God, and the civil rights, secured to us in common with other citizens, to obey our faith, in all things, & to chuse that manner of life which we believe to be the most acceptable to God and most profitable to the spiritual and temporal good of ourselves and others;— And moreover, it being our faith, that the union and relation of the Church of God in one joint-interest, is a situation the most acceptable to God, and productive of the greatest good of any state or situation attainable on earth;— Therefore, in obedience to our own faith, we have dissolved every band and tie of the flesh or fallen nature of this lost world, and covenanted and agreed as brethren and sisters in the gospel, to gather together & unite in one body as a religious community; to be constituted, built up and established upon the principles and rules of the Church of Christ aforesaid. And as God, according to his promise, has begun to give his people one heart & one way, that they may serve him forever; we do therefore expressly agree to and with each other, that the order of God made known in the Church we will observe and keep, as delivered to us, with all and singular the rules, manners and customs of the Church, in relation to union, communion and fellowship; the rights and privileges of the members, as also offices of trust and care, in the disposal and management of the joint-interest of the Church, according to the following articles of covenant.

I. We severally and jointly agree to gather ourselves together, and be constituted in the form and order of a Church, at present under the guardianship and care of John Meacham & Lucy Smith, as our spiritual parents.

II. That as it is fit and proper that certain individuals should be intrusted with the care of the temporal interest of the Church, as trustees or agents; we do therefore call, appoint and ordain three of our brethren, viz; John Bryant, Abram Wilhoit & Francis Voris to the said office of trustees or agents of the Church, mutually promising and covenanting to and with the said brethren, that they are duly invested with the said office of trustees or agents, and empowered to exercise all the duties thereof, according to the rules and regulations of the Church heretofore known and practised, and which are herein after briefly stated.

III. All who are received as members of the Church, are to be of lawful age to act for themselves, and to offer themselves freely and voluntarily, as a religious duty and according to their own faith and desire, and such as have property, and are free from debt or any just demand from those that are without, are allowed, according to their own faith, to bring in and devote, as a part of the joint-interest of the Church, all such property as they justly hold, and have an indisputable right to as their lawful interest; and the joint-interest of the Church thus formed and established by the free-will offerings of the members respectively, shall be possessed by the whole body jointly, as their natural and religious right; that is, all and every individual of or belonging to the Church shall enjoy equal rights and privileges in the use of all things pertaining to the Chh. according to their order and as every one has need, without any difference being made on account of what any one brought in; & it shall be the duty of all the members, to support and maintain the joint-interest of the Church, according to their several abilities, as members one of another, each in his or her order improving the manifold gifts of God for the good of the whole.

IV. That previous to becoming a member of the Chh. or subscribing to this covenant, those who have immediate heirs, as children, must have settled with such of them as are of lawful age, by giving or offering to them at least what the law requires as an acknowledgment, & as much more as they think proper to give them, and if convenient, require a discharge from them. And if they have children that are under age, they are to make a reserve of property sufficient to make a settlement with them in like manner, such reserve being clearly stated in writing wherein the trustees or agents of the Church shall be obligated and bound to settle with them accordingly, as they become of age; the Church having the use of such property until the time of such settlement.

V. That it shall be the duty of the trustees or agents aforesaid, to take the general charge and oversight of all and singular the property, estate and interest dedicated, devoted and given up, as aforesaid, to the joint-interest of the Church,—with all gifts, grants or donations, that may at any time be given or devoted for the benefit of the Church, or for the relief of the poor or any such charitable use or purpose; and the said joint-interest, estate, gifts, grants and donations shall be held by them, in the capacity of trustees, or agents, and shall be and remain forever, inviolably, under the care and oversight, & at the disposal of the trustee or agentship of the Church, in a continual line of succession. And we do by these presents, covenant, promise and agree, that all the transactions of the trustees or agents, in the use and disposal of the joint-interest of the church, shall be for the mutual benefit of the Church, & in behalf of the whole body, & to no personal end or purpose whatever.

But the trustees or agents shall be at liberty, in union with the body, to make presents & bestow deeds of charity upon such as they may consider the proper objects, that are without. And when by death or other means, any trustee or agent shall cease to act in his office as aforesaid, then all and singular the power vested in, and duties incumbent upon him, shall be transferred to and devolve upon his successor who shall be appointed to fill his place in said office and trust; so that each individual appointed to the office of trustee, or agent of the church, shall be vested with the power and authority of managing & disposing of the property and interest of the Chh. as aforesaid, and of making all lawful defense for the security and protection of the joint-interest and privileges of the church, and all the transactions of such members shall be valid, so long as they act in the official capacity of trustees or agents, in union with the body, according to the tenor of this covenant, and no longer.

V. And further, we covenant and agree, that it shall be the duty of the trustees to keep, or cause to be kept in a *book* or *books*, provided for that purpose, a true copy of this covenant, together with all other records or matters of a public nature, that may be necessary for the information and satisfaction of all concerned, and for the security of the join -interest of the church, committed to their care. And furthermore, that the trustees shall make application to the proper authority, for this covenant to be duly recorded in the county office of this county, together with the names of all the subscribers, who previously shall have subscribed to it; and all deeds wills. grants, &c. which may thereafter be given or conveyed to the trustees or agents aforesaid, for or in behalf of the joint-body or church, express reference shall

A NOTE TO THE READER:

It is obvious that there is textual matter missing from this reprint. It was also missing in the original: following page 84 in the only copy of this article available to us was a duplication of the Public Notice which is appended to the previous article. Otherwise, this article is an exact replication of the original.

THE CHURCH-COVENANT,
EXECUTED
At Watervliet December 7th 1818.

STATE OF OHIO MONTGOMERY COUNTY.

WHEREAS we the subscribers, denominated by each other Believers in Christ, having received the testimony of the gospel through the ministration of the Church, known by the name of Shakers, at New-Lebanon, in the township of Canaan, county of Columbia and state of New-York; and believing, according to the distinguishing faith of said Church, that Christ hath actually made his appearance the second time without sin unto salvation, and has begun to establish his kingdom of righteousness and peace on earth, which is free to all people and will stand forever; and being made partakers of that power of God, which hath called and enabled us to take up a full and daily cross against the world, the flesh, & all evil in our knowledge, and to follow Christ in the regeneration, by which, we believe, God, according to his everlasting promise, will gather together into one all things in Christ, which are in heaven and upon earth, and having taken sufficient time and precaution to prove our faith, and being fully satisfied that it is the faith of the only true gospel, into which we are called; and feeling it to be our duty and privilege, according to the Scriptures, the present call of God, and the civil and religious rights, secured to us in common with other citizens, to obey our faith, in all things, & to chuse that manner of life which we believe is most acceptable to God and most profitable to the spiritual and temporal good and welfare of ourselves and others; And being fully persuaded, that the union and relation of the Church of God in one joint-interest, is the most pleasing to God, and productive of the greatest good of any thing attainable on earth;——————And according to our faith, having entered into a covenant to gather together and be constituted as a *Family* or *Branch* of the Church at Union Village, holding one joint-interest according to the gospel; which covenant for upwards of three years hath been strictly kept and maintained; and being well satisfied, from experience, that the principles thereof are according to the true spirit of the gospel, and must stand good, both in law and conscience, according to the true sense and meaning thereof; and feeling it to be our duty and privilege, according to the increase of order in the church, to renew and confirm the said covenant, with such improvements as may be necessary for the present and future security of our rights and privileges: Therefore, we do, by these presents, covenant and agree, to renounce & disannul every band, tie and relation of the flesh, and to hold ourselves free and separate from all that pertains to the corrupt generation of fallen man; and as brethren and sisters in the gospel, to support and maintain the form, order, & relation of the church, as a branch thereof, under the immediate care and oversight of our beloved brethren, James Patterson and Nathaniel Taylor, as helps in the ministry, in union with David Darrow and Ruth-Farrington, whom we acknowledge as our spiritual parents in the work of regeneration and redemption, duly authorized & qualified, by the gift of God, to minister the only gospel of salvation to us, And whereas, thro' the faithful discharge of their ministerial duties, we have received and been plainly taught the faith and order of the Church, in relation to the rights and privileges, lots and callings, gifts and duties of the members, with the rules, manners and customs of the Church, in support of the unity, purity and peace of the body; and also the principles and practice of the Church, in relation to the care, management, use and disposal of the joint-interest of the Church, all which, we are fully satisfied, is according to the mind and will of God recorded in the Scriptures; Therefore, it is our faith and mutual agreement to ratify and confirm our covenant-engagements, to keep and maintain the faith and order, the principles and practice, and the rules, manners and customs of the Church, as delivered to us, and in particular, to hold ourselves under sacred obligations to each other strictly to observe the following Articles of agreement.

 I. We severally and jointly promise and agree to obey our parents in the Lord, for this is right;—to honor our Father and Mother, which is the first commandment with promise; to be subject to their counsel, reproof, correction and instruction in righteousness—and to observe all things whatsoever they have commanded us; to respect our brethren in spiritual care according to their gift and calling, to be faithful in our respective duties, and to keep the unity of the spirit, in the bond of peace.

II. That as it is fit and proper that certain individuals should be intrusted with the care of the temporal interest of the Church, as deacons or trustees; and as Peter Pease and others have heretofore acted in that capacity, for the security and disposal of the joint-interest of this branch of the Church, we jointly agree, that all just & lawful transactions of the deaconship hitherto, be considered and supported as valid, and that such individuals as may hereafer be called to that office and trust, be chosen according to the order of the Church, and set apart by the Ministry, through whom they are accountable to the body for all their official transactions. And being, by the union of the body, called, appointed, and set apart to the said office of deacons or trustees, they shall be considered as duly authorized and empowered to exercise all the duties thereof, according to the rules and regulations of the Church, heretofore known and practised, and which are hereinafter briefly stated.

III. All who are received as members of the Church, are to be of lawful age to act for themselves, and to offer themselves freely and voluntarily, as a religious duty and according to their own faith and desire, and such as have property, and are free from debt or any just demand from those who are without, are allowed, according to their own faith, to bring in and devote, as a part of the joint-interest of the Church, all such property as they hold justly, and have an indisputable right to as their lawful interest; and the joint-interest thus formed and established, free from debt or blame, by the free-will offerings of the members respectively, shall be possessed by the whole body jointly, as their natural and religious right; that is, each and every member of or belonging to this branch of the Church, shall enjoy equal rights and privileges in the use of all things pertaining to this branch of the Church, according to his or her calling and needs (so long as he or she remain obedient to the order and government of the Church) without any distinction being made on account of what any one brought in; and all the members are likewise holden and in duty bound to maintain and support the joint-interest, in union & conformity to the order and government of the Church, all, in their respective callings, improving their gifts and talents for the general good.

IV. That it shall be the duty of the deacons or trustees of the Church, to have the charge and oversight of all and singular the property, estate and interest dedicated, devoted and given up, as aforesaid, to the joint-interest of the Church, with all gifts, grants & donations, which may at any time be given or devoted for the benefit of the Church, or for the relief of the poor or any such charitable use or purpose; and the said joint-interest, estate, gifts, grants and donations shall be held by them, in the capacity of deacons or trustees, and shall be and remain forever, under the lawful protection, care and oversight, of the deaconship of the Church, in a continual line of succession. — And we do by these presents, mutually covenant, promise and agree, that all the transactions of the deacons in the use & disposal of the joint-interest of the Church, shall be for the mutual benefit of the Church and in behalf of the whole body, and to no personal or private end or purpose whatever.

And as it is not our design, in supporting a joint-interest, to lay up a treasure of this world's goods, but what is justly redeemed and consecrated to God, to use and improve to his honor and glory; therefore, it is our faith and agreement, never to bring into the joint-interest of the Church, by purchase or otherwise, any property which is not redeemed and free from all claim of debt or demand: and in all the transactions of the deacons or trustees, we mean that this rule be strictly observed, not to bind themselves by any obligation or promise, which would be considered as bringing the joint-interest into debt. And should any one, in the name of a deacon or trustee, or under any pretence whatever, contract any debt, on the pretended credit of the joint-interest of the Church, we shall not consider ourselves bound to answer it, but the individual shall be considered as out of union

with us, and personally accountable for his contracts.—
And furthermore, as it is our faith not to bring debt or
blame against the Church for any of our transactions, &
as we personally hold no legal claim to any part of the
consecrated property of the Church; therefore, no deacon or trustee hath any right or authority to use the joint-interest of the church, in paying any debt or damage, or answering any demand that may come against any of us, as individuals; but in all cases it shall be the duty of the deaconship, to see that the consecrated interest of the church, be appropriated to the purposes to which it is consecrated. And as it is the order and manner of the church, that all matters relating to the joint-interest of the church, be transacted in union with the body, therefore, according to this rule, the deaconship of the Chh. is, and shall be at all times, duly authorized to manage and dispose of the property and interest of the Church, in behalf of the body, and to make all lawful defense for the security of the rights and privileges of the church, according to the principles of union herein expressed.

V. And further, we covenant and agree, that it shall be the duty of the Deacons to keep, or cause to be kept in a *book* or *books*, provided for that purpose, a true copy of this covenant, together with all other records or matters of a public nature, which may be necessary for the information and satisfaction of all concerned, and for the security of the joint-interest of the church, committed to their care.

VI. *And moreover, as the whole end and design of our thus uniting in church-relation is, to receive and diffuse the manifold gifts of God, to the mutual comfort & happiness of each other, as brethren and sisters in the gospel: and, for the relief of the poor, the widow and fatherless, and such as may be deem'd real objects of charity:—Therefore, according to the faith, order & example of the Church, we do by these presents solemnly covenant, with each other, for ourselves, our heirs and assigns, never, hereafter, to bring debt or demand against the deacons of the church, nor against their successors, or any member of the Church, jointly or severally, on account of any of our services or property thus devoted and consecrated to the aforesaid sacred and charitable uses. And this covenant shall be a sufficient* witness for us before all men, and in all cases relating to the possession, order, and use of the joint-interest of the Church. And in confirmation of all the aforesaid statements, covenants, promises & articles of agreement, we have respectively, hereunto subscribed our names, beginning on this seventh day of December, in the year of our Lord 1818. In presence of each other, and of disinterested witnesses.

A Covenant-Hymn, dated U. V, Sep. 18, 1813

This hymn was publicly used in the Church, both at Union Village and Pleasant Hill, so that no room was left for any to say that the covenant was not well understood.

COME ye souls that are sincere, the gospel to pursue
Now your faith you may declare, & what you mean to do
    Are you pleas'd with what is done,
      To introduce Emanuel's reign?
Yea I am, and each for one, may freely say–Amen.

2. Can you in this work rejoice, because it saves from sin?
Was it your delib'rate choice that freely bro't you in?
    Is it your good faith alone
      That holds you like a golden chain?
Yea it is, and each for one, may freely say,–Amen.

3. Does the cov'nant you have sign'd a right'ous thing
Is it your unwav'ring mind, in it to persevere? (appear?
    In its bonds however tight
      Are you determin'd to remain
Yea I am.–Then we'll unite and jointly say Amen.

4. You have promis'd and agreed, a daily cross to bear,
And obey your gospel lead, with faithfulness and care
    Do you think it just and fit,
      A due subjection to maintain?
That's my faith, and I'll submit–and all may say, Amen

5. You have parents in the Lord, you honor and esteem
But your equals to regard, a greater cross may seem.
    Where the gift of God you see,
      Can you consent that it should reign?
Yea I can, and all that's free may jointly say,–Amen.

6. Can you part with all you've got, & give up all concern,
And be faithful in your lot, the way of God to learn?
  Can you sacrifice your ease,
  And take your share of toil and pain?
Yea I can, and all that please, may freely say,–Amen.

7. Can you into union flow, and have your will subdu'd.
Let your time & talents go, to serve the gen'ral good?
  Can you swallow such a pill—
  To count old Adam's loss your gain?
Yea I can, and yea I will, and all may say, Amen.

8. Are you properly appris'd, that in this final call,
All that you have sacrific'd, is settled once for all?
  Can you fix a final seal
  To what you cov'nant and agree?
Yea I can and all who feel, may say, so let it be.

9. what shall then be done with those who by transgresion
when they wickedly propose, their off'rings to recal (fall
  Can you treat their high demands
  As sacralegious false and vain?
Yea I can with both my hands, and justice says, Amen.

10. I set out to bear my cross, and this I mean to do:
Let old Adam kick and toss, his days will be but few,
  We're devoted to the Lord,
  And from the flesh we will be free;
Then we'll say with one accord, Amen, so let it be.

THE ORDINATION OF A TRUSTEE.

BE IT REMEMBERED, That on the twenty-second day of August, in the year of our Lord one thousand eight hundred and twenty-nine, the undersigned, constituting the Ministry of the United Society of people called Shakers, residing at Pleasant Hill, in the county of Mercer and state of Kentucky, by & with the advice of the several Elders, and also the general approbation of the members of said Society, Have and do, by these presents, ordain, call, and appoint John R. Bryant to the office of agent or trustee of the temporalities of said Society, in the room of Francis Voris who has resigned said trust: Hereby, according to the rules and regulations of the said Society, and in virtue of the authority thereby vested in us, constituting and installing the said John R. Bryant as agent and trustee of the temporal interests and concerns of the Society aforesaid, in as full and ample a manner, to the same extent, and with the same power and authority that was conferred upon the said Francis Voris, by the original covenant of said Society, bearing date the 2nd day of June, in the year 1814, and which has, heretofore been used and exercised by him, in the management of the temporal affairs of said Society.

Done at Pleasant Hill on the day, month and year first above written

SAMUEL TURNER,
ANNA S. COLE,
HOPEWEL CURTIS.

Note. The above document was drafted by counsellor Cunningham of Harrodsburg; and was adopted as an appropriate form at Union Village.

ERRATA *in some copies.*

Page 83, line 4, after *from,* read debt, or
—— 91, —6, for *the members respectively,* r. individuals
—— 92, 16, dele *estate.*
—— 93, 19, after *security,* r and protection

GENERAL RULES

OF

THE UNITED SOCIETY,

AD

SUMMARY ARTICLES OF MUTUAL AGREEMENT AND RELEASE:

RATIFIED AND CONFIRMED, BY THE SOCIETY AT WATERVLIET, MONTGOMERY COUNTY, OHIO, JANUARY, 1833.

"For all people will walk every one in the name of his God; and we will walk in the name of the Lord our God forever and ever. —And the Lord shall reign over us in Mount-Zion, from henceforth, even forever." Micah iv, 5, 7.

WHEREAS we the subscribers, members of the United Society of Believers, otherwise called Shakers, at Watervliet, in the county of Montgomery, and state of Ohio, being associated together as a religious community; in order to the mutual and permanent enjoyment of our civil and religious rights, guarantied to all the citizens of these United states, by the free constitution and equal laws of the land, and for the information of all concerned, with regard to the rules & principles of the institution, and the legal tenure by which the Church in particular, and the Society in general hold and improve their temporal property & estate, and transact their temporal business, Do, by these presents, enter into the following Articles of social and mutual agreement, to wit:—

I. We mutually agree, that we and each of us, male and female, have an undoubted and inalienable right and liberty given us of Almighty God, of believing according to our own conviction, and of acting according to our own faith—of chusing our own religion, and of giving or withholding our property or services for the support of it, as we may think proper—of worshipping God according to the dictates of our own consciences, and of acting in such a manner, in our temporal economy, as we believe will be most conducive to our own good and that of others.

II. *It is understood, mutually agreed, & declared,* That this United Society, in its spiritual and temporal establishment and economy, has its origin and foundation in a living ministry standing in a parental gift, emanating from the parent institution of the Society;—That it is the duty of the Ministry, and pertains to their proper gift, to teach and support the faith and principles, rules and orders of the Church and Society—to nominate & appoint the several official characters in the care and management of the spiritual and temporal concerns of the community, and that, by and with the general approbation and union of the Church, or of the families concerned, the said official characters become established and confirmed in their respective offices, until the said appointments be changed or revoked, by the same authority, and the same general union and approbation. That Elders are appointed to the spiritual duties of example and instruction, and Deacons are appointed to the care and management of the temporal concerns of the Church and Society, in their several lots & orders. That Trustees are appointed, to receive, hold, use, improve and appropriate all gifts, grants, and donations which are or may be bestowed and surrendered to the consecrated use, benefit, and support of the institution. That the said Trustees are authorised and empowered to hold right, title & claim, in behalf of the Church, to all and singular the lands, tenements, & hereditaments, property and estate, consecrated as aforesaid to the use and benefit of the Church, and the charitable purposes of the gospel; and to make all lawful defence (so far as consistent with the faith and principles of the Church) for the protection & security of the said united & consecrated interest, and to use and improve the same to the benefit of the Church, and to such other charitable purposes as may be deemed necessary and proper;—That the said Trustees are required to make a just and equal distribution of the said consecrated interest, for the accommodation, support, and comfort of the several families and individuals of the Church, according to their several needs and circumstances; and to bestow deeds of charity on such as may be deemed proper objects; but the said Trustees are in no wise, to alienate the said consecrated property, nor any part thereof, to any selfish, personal, or private end or purpose:—And, that said Trusteeship be perpetuated by a succession of members, appointed as aforesaid to that office, as occasion may require.

III. *It is further understood, and mutually agreed,* That the said United Society, considered at large, is composed of various orders or families:—That each family, or order, is located as different degrees of knowledge & experience and other circumstances may render proper: —That each order stands in a separate and distinct relation, with regard to their temporal interests and concerns, managements, dealings, and responsibilities; and that all dealings, business transactions, and settlements pertaining to any of the said several orders or families, are transacted with the Trustees, or proper agents in the temporal concerns and charge of the same.

IV. *It is further understood, & mutually agreed,* That the order denominated the Church, is composed of adult persons of sufficient knowledge and experience, of good moral character; free from debt, or any legal involvement, and who freely and voluntarily consecrate and devote themselves and services with all their temporal interest to the service of God, and the united support of one consecrated interest;—That no one can be admitted as a member of this order who holds any personal property or private interest;—That no property can be received and mixed or united with the consecrated interest of the Church, which is subject to any private or personal claim or demand, by reason of debt or any obligation or involvement whatever;—That no distinction is to be made, in the mutual enjoyment of the said consecrated interest, on account of what any one may have contributed to the same; & that such as contributed nothing, are equally entitled to all the common privileges & enjoyments of other members, while they continue in that order, and subject to the government thereof.

V. *It is further understood, and mutually agreed,* That the junior order is constituted for the reception, tuition and protection of young Believers,—That it is founded on the consecrated premises of the Church, under the care and superintendance of church-members, and supported, as far as may be necessary, rom the church-interest;—That into this order young Believers are admitted on trial.—If they be able and willing to work, their services are to be gratuitous & voluntary, without wages or hire:—If they have property or money, they may put it to use, for the mutual benefit of the family, without interest or usury;—it is to be valued and entered on an inventory and put into the care of the Trustees of the Church, who are bound to return it in full value at any time within 60 days after it shall be demanded: —That the property and services of this probationary class, are voluntarily appropriated to their mutual support, and any reciprocal services, gifts or donations between that order and the Church, are to be gratuitous, on both sides, without debt or demand.

VI, *It is further understood, and mutually agreed*—— That it is a well-known, established and invariable rule in the Church and Society, that no one who is admitted as a member, is ever charged for boarding, washing, lodging, clothing, nursing, or any of the enjoyments of life; that all are treated as brethren and sisters, children of one family, mutually partaking of the bounties of a kind parentage, and therefore;—It is a rule as well known and as invariable, that no person can be admitted as a member of the Society with any expectation, or upon the condition of receiving any wages or hire, as a remuneration for any labor or services rendered, (the labors, services, and benefits of members being as freely reciprocated as received) That no professed member can ever hold or bring any charge of debt, blame, or demand whatever against any agent or steward or Trustee, in particular; or against the Society in general, on account of any labor or service, or any gift, present, grant or donation, voluntarily bestowed to the uses and purposes of the institution, or for the benefit of any branch of our general community.

VII. *It is further understood, mutually agreed, and declared*, That the order denominated the Church originated, has been supported, and is perpetuated, according to the following facts and general principles; viz. That a number of families and individuals adjacent to each other, becoming identified in point of religious faith and worship, were induced, as a matter of faith & conscience, to identify also their temporal interest, which, according to the laws of the land, could not be done otherwise than by virtue of a legal covenant, specifying the agreement of the parties as to the condition in which their property should be placed, and the uses and purposes to which it should be applied. By this agreement the property was mixed and consecrated to the joint use, benefit and support of the several parties agreeing and uniting, and for other purposes: And by their union and agreement, the legal right, title, claim, control and disposal thereof was vested in Trustees appointed and authorized, by and with the assent, consent and mutual argeement of the parties so covenanting.— That the very idea of appointing Trustees, and fixing bounds and limits to their authority and control over said property, implied the existence of Trustors, who could be no other than the individuals covenanting together and placing their property in that condition.— That altho each individual relinquished his or her personal claim to what he or she might have contributed or devoted to the united interest, yet it was never meant that their equitable ownership, in their corporate capacity, was conveyed or surrendered to a Trusteeship, or that by any legal right, title, power, or authority vested in the Trustees, the authority of the Trustors was nullified, or the covenant rights and equal privileges of the members in the least impaired:—That when conveyances of real estate were made to the Trustees and their successors, for the use and benefit of the Church or community, it was clearly understood, that the persons composing that community were the real proprietors of that interest, & not the trustees individually, who merely held the fee of it for them and in their behalf

—That the interest thus conveyed, confirmed and warranted to the Church forever, through their Trustees, in a continual line of succession, is intangible by any existing law of the land;—That it only remains, to perpetuate the existence of the body, and of those fundamental articles of covenant, which identify it, in present tense, with its primary existence; Therefore,

VIII, And lastly. In conformity to the preceding facts and principles, *WE mutually agree*, That whereas the whole end and design of our thus associating ourselves together as a religious communiy, is, to receive and freely diffuse the manifold gifts of God, both of a spiritual and temporal nature, to the mutual comfort & happiness of each other, as brethren and sisters of one parentage and of one interest in the gospel, and to other benevolent purposes: *WE*, therefore, and each of us mutually, jointly and severally, *DO* promise and agree to conduct ourselves in a peaceable and orderly manner, according to the precepts of the gospel, & the rules and manners commonly known and approved in the society or family of which we are members;—that we will labor at all times, according to our several abilities, to support and build up the cause of the Society,—to discharge our respective duties,—to be kind to each other, in sickness and in health, and in all respects to make each other equal sharers in all the necessaries and comforts of life, according to the needs and circumstances of each. And having, jointly or severally, according to our respective lots, callings, orders and abilities, contributed more or less to the use, benefit, and up-building of the Church or Society in this place. *WE do*, by these presents, solemnly covenant with each other, for ourselves, our heirs and assigns, never hereafter, to bring debt or demand against the Deacons of the Church, nor against their successors, nor against any member of the Church or Society, on account of any of our property or services thus devoted and consecrated to the aforesaid sacred and charitable purposes. And these Articles shall be a sufficient witness for us before all men & in all cases relating to the condition, possession, order, and use of the temporal interest of the Church and Society. *In Testimony whereof we have hereunto set* our hands and affixed our seals on and after the fifteenth day of January, in the year of our Lord one thousand eight hundred and thirty three.

IN PRESENCE OF EACH OTHER.

Sisters' Names.	Brethren's Names.
Salome Dennis,	L S Issachar Bates,
Eunice Bedle,	Richard M· Namer,
Malinda Kitchell,	Robert Baxter,
Betcy Milligan,	Ashbel Kitchell,
Eliza Davis,	Henry Miller
Peggy Naylor,	James Ball,
Mary-Ann Duffey,	William Phillips,
Jane Patterson,	James Milligan,
Rachel Zane,	Alex. Hughey,
Caty Eastwood,	David Grummon,
Eleanor Jackson,	Thomas Wilcams,
Kezia Hughey,	John Rue.
Elizabeth Simonton	James x Martin,
Esther Ball,	Jonn L. Eastwood,
Elizabeth Maxson,	James x Grummon
Esther Eastwood,	John x Maxson,
Peggy Patterson,	John Davis,
Matilda Rue,	David Price,
Polly Dewitt,	Sam.l Tuthill,
Betsy Eastwood,	John M. Eastwood,
Matilda Williams,	Noah x Spofford,
Edith Gee,	William Slater,
Polly Ball,	Daniel x M· Lane,
Sally Kimal,	Isaac Houston,
Jane Gallaghar,	James M. Patterson,
Hannah Mayze,	Alvah West,
Frances Silence,	David Eastwood.
Polly § Rice.	
Abbey x Rice,	
Nancy x Rice. &c	&c..

A REVISION AND CONFIRMATION

OF

THE SOCIAL COMPACT

OF THE

UNITED SOCIETY

CALLED

SHAKERS,

AT

PLEASANT HILL, KENTUCKY.

"Have respect unto the Covenant: for the dark places of the earth are full of the habitations of cruelty."—DAVID.

PUBLISHED BY ORDER OF THE CHURCH.

HARRODSBURG, KY.
PRINTED BY RANDALL AND JONES.
1830

MANY erroneous opinions have been entertained concerning the Society called Shakers, calculated to mislead the public mind, in respect to the fundamental principles, rules and orders of the institutution, and it is not unfrequent that those errors are brought into Courts of Justice and there sanctioned by *exparte* testimony, the most indubitable evidence of fact to the contrary notwithstanding. Perhaps too much credit has been given to certain characters who have been members of the Society, supposing that, from experience they were capable of stating facts; not considering that through disaffection they might misrepresent the Society, not only in the circles of private life but even on the solemn ground of legal testimony. Therefore with a view to correct erroneous opinions, and as far as possible to remove prejudices and false impressions, we are induced from a sense of duty, to lay before the public the following concise statement of the general articles of agreement solemnly subscribed and ready to be attested by hundreds whose moral character stands unimpeached, as far as they are known. Should it contribute to the suppression of falsehood and the promotion of truth and justice, our object will be answered. Our highest wish is that the primary principles, rules and mutual agreements on which the institution is based be correctly understood.

REVISION AND CONFIRMATION.

Whereas, by an act of the legislature of this State dated February 11th 1828, the Society of people called Shakers is represented as living together and holding their property in common, and as such that it shall and may be lawful to commence and prosecute suits, obtain decrees and have execution against them; And whereas, by virtue of said act, sundry suits have been commenced, by persons having no just claims against the Society, whereby the Society has been involved in various troubles and aggrievances incompatible with the common rights and privileges of citizens of a free State; And, whereas, in the prosecution of those suits, founded on the aforesaid act, attempts have been made to prove that each and all who are in any way or manner connected with said Society, hold equal claims to the consecrated interest and property thereof, without regard to any rule or agreement of the Church or Society, in consequence of which, apostates from the Society have made forcible entry on the consecrated premises of the Church, and in a riotous manner seized and abused consecrated property, contrary to all laws human and divine, and moreover, on the same ground of a common tenancy, contumacious and unruly persons have forcibly maintained their claims to equal rights of possession as members, in defiance of all rules, stipulations and authorities of the institution.—Therefore in order to hold forth, to the civil and judcial authorities of the country, the proper grounds of our claim as a religious Society, to equal laws and equal protection: We the undersigned members of the united Society called Shakers at Pleasant Hill, in the County of Mercer and State of Kentucky, being associated together in the several orders of a Gospel Church and Society of Believers, *Do hereby make known to all whom it may concern*, our general principles and terms of association, and the special and particular articles of agreement solemnly subscribed, observed and maintained, in every branch of our general community touching our social and mutual rights, privileges and duties in our associated capacity and the possession, use and improvement of our temporal interest, property and estate, all which may be summed up and briefly comprised in the following particulars:

FIRST.—We unitedly agree that all men have a right to believe according to their own conviction and to act according to their own faith, being amenable to the laws of the land, that obedience to our Creator and the everlasting welfare of souls are the leading motives to our embracing and maintaining the present testimony of the Gospel and adopting our present manner of life; that we are and ever have been at full liberty to live in a private family capacity, to acquire property and to use it at our own discretion, as long as it might be our choice so to do, without any censure or breach of union on that account; that no one is compelled by any rule of the Society to devote to the common benefit of the institution, either property, time or service, beyond or contrary to his or her own faith and free choice; that it is not according to the rules, manners and customs of the society, for any one to live idly on the property or labor of others; that no one be allowed to consecrate or bestow property to the Society, in any manner that would defraud creditors or natural heirs, or to amalgamate his property and services with the consecrated interest of the Church, until he has had sufficient time and opportunity, in a junior order, to become acquainted with the rules, manners and general orders of the Church; that in this junior or probationary order the junior members of the Society may convene together and live in a joint family relation, holding their property separate and disconnected from that of the Church; that each and all the members of such family shall have the privilege of taking an inventory of all the money and property that each may choose to put into the possession of the Deacon or Steward of the family, said property being first valued by men chosen for that purpose; that any member of such family choosing to remove and separate from said family shall be entitled to all the money and property which he or she deposited as aforesaid, of which the said inventory shall determine the amount; and the said Deacon or Steward shall be forthcoming for the same, in articles of the same kind and value or equivalent thereto; the said money and property to be delivered within six months after due notice is given of such removal or sooner if convenient. But the uses and benefits of all such money and property with all the labor and service which may be done or rendered in any place or for any person, and all gifts or donations freely bestowed for the benefit of the family or Society, during the residence of the individual in such family, are freely devoted and consecrated to the benevolent purposes of the institution, and no member of such family shall ever bring any charge of debt, damage or demand against the family or Society or any member thereof for any money, property, labor or service, given, rendered or devoted as aforesaid to the support or convenience of the said family or Society, nor any reckoning be required otherwise than according to the aforesaid inventories or other written agreements acknowledged by the Deacon or Steward of the family. That, on the other hand, the family or Society shall make no account nor hold any demand against any individual member for any money, property or service given, rendered or furnished for his or her support or convenience, in sickness or in health; that all the members shall share jointly and equally in all the privileges and in the use of all things possessed by said family, according to their several needs, without any difference being made on account of what any one brought in: That the members unitedly agree to live

A

in union with each other and in obedience to the rules and regulations of the family, and those who may have the care and management thereof; and that these articles be considered valid and of full force in law, as far as they respect law, and the subscribers to be admitted as lawful witnesses of the same: That in this junior order any or all are permitted to continue during life, provided it be their choice so to do, but when it becomes, the faith and desire of individuals of the Society to step forward into Church order and the way is prepared for their admission they must then settle it in their hearts to make a full sacrifice to God, once for all, as no ground is or can be left for any recantation or drawback.

SECOND.—All who are admitted into church order assent, consent and agree, that they have taken sufficient time and precaution to prove their faith;—that they are fully persuaded that it is the faith of the only true gospel into which they are called;—that it accords with the Holy Scriptures and the present call of God to them;—that it is consistent with the civil and religious rights guaranteed by the laws of the land to obey it in all things: that they believe the union and relation of the church in one interest to be preferable to any other state or order of society;—That this order, being spiritual, requires them to relinquish that which is carnal,—to abandon the common course and spirit of the world;—to devote themselves wholly to the service of God, in a life of piety and virtue:—to cross and deny their own self-will and evil inclinations, and submit to the rules, manners and customs of the church, in all things, as heretofore known and practised. Hence it is the agreement of all who are acknowledged as church members, that the church is constituted under the general care of a standing Ministry whose nomination and appointment is sanctioned and supported by the primary or parental authority of the society:—That it belongs to the Ministry to teach and support the rules and orders of the church;—to appoint the several agents or official characters for the care and management of the concerns of the church both spiritual and temporal: that trustees are appointed to receive, hold, use and appropriate all gifts, grants and donations which are given and devoted to the joint use, benefit and support of the institution; that the said trustees are under proper limits & restrictions in all their official transactions; that they are required to make a just and equal distribution of the consecrated property to all the several families of the Church, according to their needs and circumstances, and bestow deeds of charity to such as may be considered proper objects, without the bounds of the church; but not to alienate any part of said consecrated interest to any personal end whatever: that the said trustees are authorized and empowered, to hold right, title and claim in behalf of the church to all and singular the lands, tenements and hereditaments, property and estate consecrated as aforesaid to the use and benefit of the church, and to make all lawful defence for the protection, security and appropriation of the same to the uses and purposes stipulated; and that said trusteeship be perpetuated by a succession of members nominated and appointed to that office as occasion may require.

THIRD.—It is further understood and agreed, that all who are received as members of the church, be of lawful age to choose and act for themselves;—that they be free from debt or any just demand from those who are without the bounds of the church: that they dispose of their property, if they have any, in such a manner as to bring nothing into the church to which in future, they can hold any personal or individual claim: that they may give or bequeath their property to their heirs, if they choose, or consecrate, as a free will offering to the church, any part that they may think proper, and thus become wholly dependent for their support, as church members, on the consecrated funds of the church, provided for the mutual and equal benefit of all that belong to that order: that by virtue of the mutual agreement of all concerned, all and every individual of or belonging to the church shall enjoy equal rights and privileges in the use of all things pertaining to the church, as every one has need, without any difference being made on account of what any one may have contributed or consecrated: and it shall be the duty of all the members to support and maintain the said consecrated interest according to their several abilities.

FURTHERMORE.—That it shall be the duty of the Trustees to keep or cause to be kept in a Book or Books provided for that purpose a true copy of this covenant, together with all other Records or matters of a public nature, that may be necessary for the information and satisfaction of all concerned and for the security of the temporalities of the church committed to their care: and in all deeds, wills, grants, &c. which may thereafter be given or executed to the trustees, in behalf of the church, express reference shall be had to the same, specifying the date or time when it was subscribed or began to be subscribed.

LASTLY.—As the whole end and design of our thus associating together as a religious community is to receive and freely diffuse the manifold gifts of God to the mutual comfort and happiness of each other as brethren and sisters in the gospel and other charitable purposes: therefore according to the faith, manner, rule, order and example of the Church and Society aforesaid, we the undersigned having jointly or severally, according to our respective lots, callings, orders, abilities and degrees of faith, consecrated and contributed more or less to the use, benefit and upbuilding of the Church or Society at Pleasant Hill aforesaid.

We do, by these presents, for ourselves our heirs and assigns exonerate, release, discharge and quitclaim to each other and also to the Deacons, agents and trustees of the Church and Society and all and every person or persons belonging to our said Church and Society of and from all charges, costs, suits, debts, damages, incumbrances and troubles whatever, on account of any property labor or service that has been or that may be given, rendered, devoted or consecrated according to the foregoing stipulations and for the aforesaid sacred and charitable uses.

In confirmation whereof, we have hereunto set our hands and affixed our seals on and after the 20th day of May, one thousand eight hundred and thirty, In presence of each other.

Number of Subscribers   210.
ATTEST,—G. R. RUNYON, J. R. BRYANT, JAMES RANKIN.

CONCLUDING REMARKS,

Extracted from a pamphlet, lately published by the Society, at New-Lebanon, N. Y.

"Having, in the preceding pages, given as concise and comprehensive account of this Society as our limits will permit, we shall conclude with a few remarks. Nothing tends more to promote the improvement of the principles of light and truth in the mind of man, than a free, candid and unprejudiced enquiry, and a willingness to examine into the truth of any principles and practices which are at variance with his natural inclinations and prepossessions. Prejudice operates upon the mind like jaundice upon the eye, which prevents it from seeing objects, except through a medium discolored by its own infirmity; and therefore it cannot form any just or correct ideas of what it does actually see. So with prejudice; it sees its object through its own disordered medium, and judges of it accordingly.

It is an unfortunate circumstance that the great mass of mankind are swayed by popular opinion, and blindly follow its current to any extreme, without consideration or reflection. The operation of popular influence upon the community, is much like the agitation of a body of water, which is disturbed and put in motion by any object thrown into it; and this agitation is always in proportion to the force and magnitude of the object. So the senses and feelings of an extensive community are often affected and set in motion by the influence of some master spirit, whose interested designs are directed to the passions and prejudices of that community. And though the public good is generally made the plea to obtain the gratification of private ambition or malice; yet whatever may be the ostensible object of the instigator, whether of a religious, politcal or any other nature, the medium of excitement is the same.—The passions are addressed, and prejudices awakened, and the effect is in proportion to the estimated importance of the object artfully held up to view. Popular clamour is raised to the highest pitch of excitement; and thus the object of the master spirit is often accomplished. And it often happens, that the prime movers of such excitments, like puppet show-men, are artfully concealed behind the curtain.

Of all the objects of excitement brought before the public, none are more calculated to make an impression on the mind of man than the subject of religion. This has been the origin of pesecution in all ages. The public mind is set in motion by designing and interested persons, against some person, principle or system of religion, which stands in the way of their ambitious designs. Such was the excitement raised by Demetrius and his interested coadjutors, against the apostle Paul, among the Ephesians, who were persuaded to believe, that through the preaching of Paul, their religion was in danger, and "that the temple of the great goddess Diana would be despised, and her magnificence destroyed;" while the real danger apprehended, was the loss of the lucrative craft of the prime movers of the tumult.

In all ages, those religious persons or sects; however few or small; who, regardless of popular opinion, have presumed to think and act for themselves, and to advocate and practice virtue, according to their own unbiassed judgment, have always been the objects of popular odium. And persecution against such has always been excited in proportion to the contrast of their principles with the present popular feelings and opinions, and the self-denial which those principles required against the inbred propensities of human nature; because such principles are viewed as obstacles in the way of the interested designs of aspiring ambition.

The only efficacious remedy against the influence of such contaminating excitements on the mind, is calm and candid consideration, a sincere and impartial enquiry after light and truth, and a dispassionate examination of every principle presented to the mind which requires important action. The action will then proceed from deliberate judgment, and not from the impulse of excited passion. In tracing the history of the human race, we rarely find a heinous crime committed under, the influence of calm consideration; but generally, if not always, under the influence of some pernicious and baneful passion; or from some corrupt principle, which has been designedly instilled into the mind conformable to those passions. All slanders proceed from this source. No wars, no tyranny nor persecution could ever be supported by any other principle. If ever the civil and religious liberties of this nation are overthrown, it will be done through the prevalence of these causes. When strenuous and unceasing efforts are continually made to gain a religious ascendancy; and to obtain the passage of laws in favor of the opinions and views of some predominant sect; which lays claim to exclusive orthodoxy, and when laws are enacted with no other design than to favor such schemes, and to operate against an unpopular sect, then let the lovers of rational liberty beware, lest the consummation of all these designs and exertions should finally terminate in the baneful and dreaded combination of the civil and ecclesiastical powers, to sway the destinies of our country. Should this once be accomplished, then adieu, an everlasting adieu to all the liberties and privileges, both civil and religious, which have hitherto been the fair and distinguished portion of this highly favored nation.

The utility of every principle and system must be tested by its nature and effects. We therefore request the reader to examine candidly, and without prejudice, the foregoing exposition of this Society; and see if he can discover any thing in the principles of its system incompatible with purity, justice and charity—any thing inconsistent with the social and spiritual happiness, or any thing which is not compatible with the free agency of man, or with those civil and religious rights bestowed upon us by our beneficient Creator, and secured by the free institutions of our country.

We are well aware that these principles require great self-denial against the natural propensities of man. But surely, if we believe the testimony of our Saviour. this can be no proof that they are not the principles of genuine christianity. But whether they are approved or disapproved, or whether they are agreeable or disagreeable to the feelings of human nature, no one can have any reasonable ground of complaint, nor any cause of opposition, since all are at their own option to embrace them or not.

The faith and principles of this Society have been tested more than fifty years in this land. Originating from means apparently the most contemptible and inadequate, and destined to stem all the opposition of nature's passions, and to confront the pride and ambition of the world, and the persecutions of the bigoted votaries of more popular religions, they have increased and grown, and been gradually unfolded and extended, and have been received by many; until they have established a people in that united order of harmony, peace and social happiness, which continues to excite the increasing attention and wonder of mankind."

INVESTIGATOR;

OR

A DEFENCE

OF

THE ORDER, GOVERNMENT & ECONOMY

OF

THE UNITED SOCIETY

CALLED

SHAKERS,

AGAINST

SUNDRY CHARGES & LEGISLATIVE PROCEEDINGS.

Addressed to the Political World.

BY THE SOCIETY OF BELIEVERS
AT PLEASANT HILL, KY.

He that is first in his own cause seemeth just; but his neighbour cometh and searcheth him.—SOLOMON.

LEXINGTON, K.
PRINTED BY SMITH & PALMER.
1828.

INTRODUCTION.

THE design of this small publication is to shed light on a subject which heretofore has been veiled in some obscurity; we mean the form and order of the United Society in a civil or political point of view. By a variety of copious publications, we have exhibited to the religious world almost every thing that relates to our faith and manners as a religious society; but as there is an external form and order in our association as a Church, related to the civil rights established by the civil institutions of our country, in order that our civil rights be not violated either through ignorance or design, it becomes necessary that all such of our social contracts, rules, manners, laws or customs, as are in any respect connected with our civil rights, should be explicitly known and correctly understood.

It is generally known that serious difficulties have, for some time past, existed in this branch of the United Society, owing to the withdrawal of certain members, who through the influence of popular or interested connections, instituted claims on the Society repugnant to all our well known covenants, rules and customs. Various were the means used to interest public sympathy on the side of the withdrawing party, if possible to substantiate those claims, which it seems could not be done under the present system of civil law; hence a petition was presented to the legislature at their last session praying for a special act to aid the party in their intended enterprize.

This act being obtained, almost the first notice we received of its existence was from a display of its authorities on our house of worship, the door being abused in posting up publick notices to the Society, of a character very unsuitable to the place. This, indeed, appeared to us a strange affair, knowing that we had ever observed the greatest punctuality in our dealings with mankind and with each other. We had constituted an office and trusteeship, for the transaction of all matters of trade and commerce abroad, and all our domestic concerns we considered as fully and finally adjusted by our own mutual contracts and articles of agreement:

it did, therefore, appear to us a mysterious thing, indeed, for the whole Society to be attacked, in a way so imposing on our religious character and sacred rights, as if the house of God had become a den of thieves, that a subpœna must be stuck up on the door calling us out, in a body, to answer the claims of justice.

From the abundant information contained in our religious publications, we could not have supposed that any respectable body of well informed citizens could have conceived of us as a political establishment. The well known principles of faith and manner of life which we have adopted sufficiently negative the idea; and how any legislative body could claim a right by special enactment to intrude into the sacred asylum of our church order is to us a mystery, seeing that, even "Congress shall make no law concerning an establishment of religion, or prohibiting the free exercise thereof."

In forming our religious association we have not consulted the civil authorities of men, further than to see that we did not trespass upon their premises. Our faith and forms of devotion were not chartered by any legislative power of a political nature. As a community of Believers we disclaim the right or privilege of suing or being sued, in a body; our main policy is to keep out of the reach of the municipal law, by strictly observing all its just requirements, and so arranging our social concerns as not to interfere with the rights and privileges of others. With this confidence we shrink not from the scrutiny of the publick or the law, on any point relating to our civil economy or social contracts, provided we be not compelled into such scrutiny by illegal and unconstitutional measures, requiring a surrender of our impartial rights, and subjection to an authority not claimed by our National Government.

The singularity of our religious profession has always dictated to us retirement from the contentions of the political world, and the conscious innocence which we labour to maintain, forbids our attention to the absurd and ridiculous charges so often peddled about through the country by those who wrongfully hate us. It is not, therefore, the slanders of a few solitary individuals, nor the popular clamours of a misinformed public that, at present, excites our attention; but the voice of those civil authorities which we ever respect, and which have been roused, by the cry of injustice, in effect, to demand of us a statement of facts with corroborating evidence from which the legality or illegality of our institution might appear, and our claims to equal rights of toleration, as a religious society, be legally decided.

From these considerations we respectfully offer to the political department of our country, whether professors of religion or nonprofessors, such information relative to the points in question, as we think, will come properly under their cognizance, including—The aforesaid petition to the legislature—The Act of the legislature founded on said petition—Objections to said Petition and Act, with reference to the decision of the legislature of Pennsylvania on a similar case—Various details and statements concerning the laws, customs and character of our Society—The decisions of sundry Courts of Justice on all the important questions that relate to our civil and social rights, &c. &c.

Petition of John Whitby and others to the Legislature.

To the Honorable the General Assembly of the Commonwealth of Kentucky.

We the undersigned petitioners feeling ourselves much aggrieved by the fraudulent conduct of those who hold the reins of government in a society of people called Shakers, residing at Pleasant Hill, Mercer county, do respectfully implore your honourable body to take our case into consideration, and if it is not inconsistent with the powers confided to you by the Constitution, we humbly pray that you may devise, in your wisdom, some plan whereby our distresses may be alleviated.

Your petitioners do solemnly declare, that some years previous to this, from honest and conscientious views, they were induced to unite themselves to that Society on certain principles which they considered were best calculated to promote their happiness. We were told by them that as the work of their institution was progressive in consequence of its members increasing in knowledge and virtue, they had no creed or articles of faith, neither any written laws by which their Society was governed. That no coercive or arbitrary measures were ever taken in the government of this Society—that conscience was entirely free, that all required of each individual was always to act honestly according to that degree of faith which he or she should at any time possess: And that usurpation of authority over the conscience, among them was never known. That each individual had an indefeasible and equal right to all property belonging to the Society, and that no member was ever expelled from the society for any cause whatever. The above stated conditions, with others of the same import, we considered to be sufficiently liberal, and when we compared them with their written publications sent abroad into the world we believed them to be true.

Under these considerations and with these views we continued with the society for some years, and by an active and laborious life, faithfully discharged what we believed to be our duty, by a willing conformity to all the rules and orders of practical life given to us by our leaders, and by these means secured to ourselves much satisfaction, until our leaders began to deviate from those principles on which we had joined them. Your petitioners do further testify, that for no other cause than a private expression of certain opinions relative to moral sentiment, which we most conscientiously believed to be not only true, but the strongest basis of pure morality, that some of us were publickly anathematized, grievously misrepresented and most peremptorily ordered to leave the society or make a recantation of our sentiments; and (to heighten the injustice of their oppression) sentiments too that would not lead to the violation of one moral precept contained in the doctrines of the society, but remove many manifest errors of which the society [i. e. the flesh] complained. The oppressive dealings towards some, and the severe threats of like abusive treatment of others, rendered us so uncomfortable that we could no longer enjoy satisfaction in the society, and were almost forced to leave the place without any compensation for our long and faithful services.

These, with many grievances too tedious to mention, have created a determination in some of us to seek redress at law; but we have been told by our counsellors that as the society of Shakers are a body without any Act of Incorporation, and as many of them stand in a very singular relation to each other in consequence of a form of covenant established among them redress at law could not easily be obtained, without first some provision being made, by an Act of your honourable body.

Therefore we humbly submit our case to your consideration, to do, as you in your wisdom, may consider most prudent. That the above statements are in substance true, we have no doubt, can easily be made appear to the full satisfaction of any court of justice in this Commonwealth.

We the undersigned citizens residing in and near the vicinity of Shakertown, being fully persuaded, according to all the information we are able to collect, that the above stated petition contains an impartial statement of facts, and feeling anxious that some law may pass whereby justice may be administered to the petitioners, do most cordially unite with those aggrieved in subscribing our names.—Floyd Burks, H. T. Deweese, Lambert Banta, James Lillard, Wm. Pherigo, Thos. Wood, Robert P. Steenbergen, jr. Josiah Utley, Abraham A. Brewer, John Rinearson, Aaron Rinearson, W. A. Bridges, Wm. T. Wood. Saml. Eccles, B. Prather, J. Smedley, Thos. Allen, Sen. Philip T. Allen, Wm. Tume, B. T. Hall.

Mr. Samuel Banta having stated to me (in which I have the utmost confidence) that in leaving the Shakers he lacks complete remedy to recover the property which he first and subsequently took to them: That they refuse satisfactory accountability, he only demanding the original sums, waiving his pretensions to interest and labor: And thinking this reasonable, if a remedy can be constitutionally devised. My belief of the personal honesty and uprightness of Samuel Banta, and that he would ask nothing improper, induces me to sign his petition. P. Trapnall, Chr. Chinn, Garret Banta, Wm. Ross, Wm. Edwards, John S. Chenowith, John Eccles, Isaac Westerfield, James Burnett, Abram V. Brewer.

With much difficulty we obtained the foregoing documents; they are without the principal signatures, we therefore add the following extracts of a private communication from the author and principal instigator of the petition.—"Being called upon by one of the Shaker friends for a copy of the petition drawn by me, and which was presented to the Legislature, containing a part of my grievances upon which a law was passed. My memory not serving me to gratify their wishes (not having reserved a copy) I, with frankness, give them the substance of my objections of grievances, so as to give them a fair opportunity of explaining to me or the world the reasons for their conduct, which was then and still is considered as oppressive and despotic." [Here he gives the detail of his treatment much as it is in the petition; and in allusion to his being called to an account by the elders, observes] "for the correcting and exposure of which error, I have been disposed to set about an inquiry, and still to prosecute it, not so much for the purpose of gain, but that a fair exposure of it shall be made. The sum total of my objections to the society was the spirit and manner of exercising this despotic oppression, through a secret counsel of the leads and elders, &c."—"The many things to which my soul stands wedded in the Shakers need not nor have time to name. JOHN WHITBEY."

What a noble subject for legislation! Seventeen names it is said were attached to the main petition, in union with this principal plaintiff, thirteen of whom had never been admitted into the fellowship of the church, and of course could have no cause of complaint except, like their leader, that they were not tacitly permitted to say and do as they pleased. As for those near neighbours of ours whose names went to corroborate the petition, with the exception of three or four (who live within the distance of four miles) they generally reside from seven to seventeen miles distant. It may also serve as a memorial of the sagacity of the managers of the affair, that no invitation was extended to us, to enter into any investigation before the committee. A trustee of the church, it is true, who happened to be present, presented a *response*, which, it seems, was but little regarded. A plan so artfully constructed was not to be frustrated with trifles. The bill, we are told, was warmly opposed by members of the first respectability. But popular prejudice!! who can penetrate its damps with the torch of reason, or even the blaze of common sense? However, we must check those freedoms of thought; and respectful of the wisdom and talent that graced the political temple of the State, introduce this singular act, and let it speak for itself.

AN act to regulate civil proceedings against certain communities having property in common.

§ 1. Be it enacted by the General Assembly of the Commonwealth of Kentucky, That it shall and may be lawful for any person having any demand exceeding the sum of fifty dollars, founded on any contract implied or expressed, against any of the communities of people called Shakers, living together and holding their property in common, to commence and prosecute suits, obtain decrees, and have execution against any such community by the name or description by which said community is commonly known, without naming or designating the individuals of such community, or serving process on them, except as is hereinafter directed, all such suits shall be by bill in chancery in the circuit court of the county in which such community resides; and it shall and may be lawful to make parties to such suits all other persons, by name, who may have any interest in the matter in controversy, or who may hold any property in trust for said community or may be indebted to them.

§ 2. When any subpœna founded on any such bill shall be placed in the hands of any officer to execute, he shall fix a copy of such subpœna on the door of the meeting-house of such community, shall deliver a copy to some known member of the community, and shall read the subpœna aloud at some one of the dwellings of said community at least ten days before the term of the court at which said community are required to answer; and on those facts being returned in substance on the subpœna they shall constitute a good service of process on said community, so as to authorise the court to require and compel an answer agreeable to the rules and usages in chancery.

§ 3. All answers for and in behalf of such community may be filed on the oath or affirmation of one or more individuals of such community, who shall moreover swear or affirm that he or they have been nominated as the agents or attorneys of such commuty to defend such suit, and thereupon the individual so swearing shall have full power and authority to manage and conduct said suit, on the part of such community, or to settle and adjust the same; and all notices to take depositions against such community may be served on such agents, or left at their place of residence: provided, that for good cause shown, the court may at any time permit such agents to be changed or substituted by others of the community; provided, however, that the agents or defendants shall not be compelled to answer on oath to any charges or allegations which are by the existing rules of law and equity cognizable alone in courts of common law—provided further, that in all such cases as mentioned in the foregoing proviso, the defendants shall be entitled to a jury if they or any one of them shall signify their desire to that effect any time before the trial shall be gone into; and in such cases as above described either party may require the personal attendance of witnesses, and a viva voce examination as though the suit were at common law, and the court shall direct such process at the request of either party, or summons may issue, as in other cases of the kind.

§ 4. Be it further enacted, that nothing in this act contained shall be so construed as to render the communities aforesaid, or either of them, liable upon contracts entered into by any individual or individuals not authorised by their laws and usages to contract for such community; nor shall it be so *construed* as to give to any person who having been a member of any such community, has heretofore left it, or may hereafter leave it, any right in consequence of such membership, which he or she would not have had if this act had not passed, but such right shall depend upon and be determined by the laws, covenants and usages of such society, and the general laws of the land, except as to the mode of the suit.

§ 5. Be it further enacted that any community which may be sued under the provisions of this act, shall have the same right to a change of venue as other defendants. Approved, Feb. 11th, 1828.

Having, now, presented, in full, the substance of this singular prosecution; that the publick may not imagine that our *Investigation* or *Defence* is offered by a nameless and irresponsible set of beings, such as the foregoing proceedings seem to be directed against, the following names, of a few responsible characters, are hereunto subscribed—in behalf of the the society.

ABRAM WILHITE,
FRANCIS VORIS,
EDMUND BRYANT,
JACOB MONTFORT,
Pleasant Hill, June 10, 1828.

JOHN R. BRYANT,
JAMES M. RANKIN,
JAMES CONGLETON
WILLIAM SHIELDS Jr

INVESTIGATOR, &c.

"Printing presses shall be free to every person who undertakes to examine the proceedings of the Legislature or any branch of Government—and every citizen may freely speak, write and print on any subject, being responsible for the abuse of that liberty."
Constitution.

OBJECTIONS TO THE PETITION OF J. WHITBEY, &c.

It is objected to said petition, That its contents were not legitimate subjects of legislation—that the supposed facts stated in it are destitute of proof, and that it contains a variety of misrepresentations.

1. To suppose, as this petitioner represents, that we have *no creed* or articles of faith, neither any written laws by which we are governed, is false. We hold out no such character of the society to induce unprincipled men to join us; it is well known that we reject *human creeds* and articles of *sectarian faith;* but our belief in all the essential doctrines of the gospel is no less public. We have no system of laws of our own making, but we have the law of Moses, and the laws of our country and the precepts of our ancestors and elders, which are all written and common in every family, according to the spirit of which our actions are regulated.

2. We hold indeed that conscience is entirely free from human control; but we have never taught that under pretence of freedom of conscience, every member of society might say and do as he pleased secure from censure or blame: The rules and orders of our institution have ever maintained all necessary control over the words and actions of members, to preserve a respectful conformity to the principles of truth and virtue established both in civil and religious society.

3. The insinuation, in said petition, that we force people to act beyond or contrary to their faith is groundless. It is true, we admit of different degrees of faith, and hold each one justified, in always acting honestly according to the degree of faith which he has attained, but we do not approve of any member turning away

from the faith and adopting the opinions of Epicurus, Voltaire, or Robert Owen, and usurping authority to disseminate those, or any other opinions repugnant to our common faith, either publicly or privately among the members of our society: and to reprove a disorderly member sharply that he may be sound in the faith, we have not considered a crime worthy of a legal prosecution. Indeed, the authorities of a just internal government adapted to check evil doers and for the praise of them that do well, we rank among our greatest blessings.

4. With regard to coercive or arbitrary measures, our public testimony is, that "in the order and government or regulation of the church, no compulsion or violence is either used, approved, or found necessary," and the petitioner has proved nothing against the church to the contrary. In the junior order where he was located such government is exercised as wisdom and prudence may dictate and the law of the land justify.

5. Respecting the rights of property we are sorry, that the petitioner so greatly erred on a subject of such importance, and that in direct contradiction to his own public statements previously made. Perhaps nothing could be more foreign from the truth than to hold out the idea that each individual ever had an indefeasible and equal right to all the property belonging to the society. This we can prove to be false from his own printed pamphlet

6. With regard to expelling members. No compulsion or arbitrary force has ever been used in that case. What the petitioner states, relative to his own case, cannot be construed so as to imply any act of violence. In his book, he details the circumstances at large; in which he shows plainly that he was the first who deviated from the terms of membership,—That he announced his belief in the system of Robert Owen; discarded the doctrine of *praise and blame, rewards and punishments, &c.*—was admonished by the Ministry and Elders not to propagate such doctrine,—refused admonition,—became contumacious and bold,—rejected all authority, and was ordered to retract what the elders called *vile stuff,* or leave the society. Admitting he was treated with some severity as a catechumen, we cannot conceive that a Legislature was the proper tribunal to dictate the means of redress.

OBJECTIONS TO THE FOREGOING ACT.

"Acts of the Legislature that are impossible to be performed are of no validity; and if there arise out of them any absurd consequences manifestly contradictory to common reason, they are with regard to those collateral circumstances void." 1 B. p. 90. Agreeably to this maxim we object to the description of our society in said act, § 1. as "living together and holding our property in common.". We know of no public record, act, matter or thing to authorise such a description, beyond the partial and incorrect statements given in the foregoing petition.

2. We object to the idea of prosecuting suits, obtaining decrees, and having execution against the whole society by the name or description by which we are commonly known. All bodies cognizable by law must, in our opinion, have a name or description by which they are known in law. Vulgar names and descriptions, without any allusion to persons, we must consider a precarious foundation for a legal process.

3. We object to the idea of making parties to such suits all other persons by name, who may have any interest in the matter, &c. however lawful this may be in common cases, considering the ground on which we are placed, by this mode of forming parties, too great a force may be enlisted against us, to afford us any ground for a legal or just defence.

4. We object to the mode of serving process described at large in sec. 2, as incompatible with our religious rights. A meeting-house known in law as "*a temple or building consecrated to the honor of God and religion,*" we deem an improper place for setting up such public notices, calculated to arrest the attention of the worshippers to improper subjects, and afford spectators occasion of conducting disrespectfully toward us, as a people under such legal impeachments. The British statutes debarred transactions, inconsistent with the place, even from the church-yard; and are our civil laws less respectful of religious rights?

5. We further object to sec. 3, as exercising an authority over our community subversive of our common rights; that is, in either admitting, as defendants in any suit, persons not duly nominat-

ed according to our rules, or compelling us to make such nomination, which we could not consistently do, without acknowledging this arbitrary act as constitutional, and the society obliged by it to change their character, conformably to its definitions. The proper persons, among us, for defending all causes actionable in a court of justice, are already nominated and known by name, whether as private individuals or public agents. It does not therefore appear to us consistent with sound policy, that we should, as a religious society, be obliged to enter into any measure not consistent with our established rules and the constitution and laws of the land.

These things considered, is it not to be regretted that the Legislature did not act with caution similar to that of the Pennsylvania Legislature at their last session in a similar case ? We allude to the petition of a number of inhabitants of the county of Beaver, relating to the celebrated society at Economy. This case was so perfectly similar to that before us, that we deem it proper to adduce the report of that committee as a striking evidence of the precipitance and partiality in the enactment against this society, as well as the unconstitutionality of its bearings.

The following extract is copied from the *Waynesburg Messenger* of Jan. 12th, 1828. " SENATE, Dec. 17th. Mr Hawkins, from the committee of the judiciary, made report, which was read as follows :—

" The judiciary committee, to whom was referred the petition of a number of the citizens of the county of Beaver, relating to the society at Economy, reported : That they have carefully examined the petitions and documents submitted to them, and have heard the statements of the representatives of the parties interested, from which they have gathered a slight knowledge of the rise, progress and present condition of the society. * * *

" With the objects of the society, or its police or regulations, your committee have derived but a very limited knowledge, except what is communicated in a document accompanying the petition of the complainants, which is altogether ex parte, and was unsupported by the oaths of those who signed it. It seems to be admitted, however, and not denied by either party, that the joint labor and the property of the society is held, or was originally intended to be held and enjoyed in common; and that George Rapp, the priest and patriarch of the company, has the supervision, control and management over all their concerns, both spiritual and temporal.

"They have formed, at different times, two several constitutions, the one at Wabash, the other at Economy, which contain provisions very similar, except that the last one is more favorable to persons disposed to withdraw. It contains in substance, the following conditions, viz. 1. That all holding property, who joined the society, put it into the common stock; and when they leave the society, they get back what they put in, without interest. 2d. Those who put no property into the society, and leave the society without leave, or giving notice to the society of their intention, their services are to be considered voluntary, and entitled to no compensation. 3d. That those who put no property into the common stock, who give notice of their intention to leave the society, and behave well, will be given something to begin the world with, the amount in the discretion of the society. Before signing this, persons having a desire for admission have a probation from six to nine months, during which time, they are instructed in the principles, rules and regulations of the society.

"Jacob Shriver (whose case gives rise to the present application) states, that he entered into this association at the age of 17, and remained among them about 20 years, when having made some discoveries, which caused him to be dissatisfied, he left them. When he entered the society, he contributed no property to the common stock; so that his claim is wholly for services rendered.

He states in the petition, "that the inhabitants are now suffering the greatest injustice and imposition, contrary to the spirit of the constitution, &c.—but does not refer to the nature of the offence against the constitution, or to any particular clause in the constitution that is violated. He also sets forth, that numbers, through ignorance have been drawn into the slavery of George Rapp, through the delusion of being joint partners of the institution; but when they wished to withdraw, they found they were mistaken, and were not allowed one cent for their services. Without presuming to affirm or deny the truth of these allegations, your committee are clearly of opinion, that they are legitimate subjects of judicial inquiry; nor have the petitioners pointed out any definite mode of relief, which could be given by the legislature. If Mr Shriver has, voluntarily, entered into a contract with Mr. Rapp individually, there can be no doubt of his obtaining redress in a court of law, if by the terms or nature of his contract, he be entitled to it; but if his agreement was with the society, whether it has been faithfully complied with or not, it is absolutely void. As a society, having no charter of incorporation, they have no legal existence, they can make no binding contract, nor can they sue or be sued.

If Mr Shriver has made a contract which has turned out to his disadvantage, it is his own fault; that contract can neither be cancelled by the legislature, nor can they create a new one for him. Besides, a suit at law has been brought, and is now pending, in the court of common pleas of Beaver county; and if no other difficulty was presented, this would seem a sufficient one, at least, for a delay of legislative interference. That he should have spent twenty years in the prime of his life in the service of the society, and then leave it, may perhaps be regarded as a serious evil; but it was one which was brought upon him by his own act. When he entered into it, he entered with a knowledge that the forfeiture of his labour would be the consequence of his withdrawal; and in consideration of his services while there, if he had remained, he was entitled, by the terms of his contract, to shelter, food and other ncessaries of life, and to be instructed in the religious opinions of their priest and ruler, Mr. Rapp.

That a society thus formed, should spring up in the bosom of a country, whose constitution and laws are based upon the equal rights of man, may seem novel and extraordinary; but that they have a right to associate in this way, by their own agreement, while they commit no overt acts of transgression against the laws of the country, cannot, perhaps, at this day be questioned. Whether the sum of human happiness is advanced, and the cause of religion and the Commonwealth promoted, by such associations, your Committee deem it improper to inquire. Neither does it seem to your Committee, to be within the scope of legislative duties, to inquire whether the society has been brought together, as has been suggested, either through superstition, ignorance or de-

sign. If it be so, the true christian and philanthropist may lament, but no power in this government can shackle the free operations of the mind, in its religious exercises, or prevent any freeman from disposing of his property or services as may seem to him right. * * *
Upon the whole, your Committee recommend the adoption of the following resolution:

Resolved, That the Committee be discharged from the further consideration of the subject.

The Senate of Pennsylvania have adopted the report delivered by Mr. Hawkins upon the petition, &c. complaining of injustice being done by Mr. George Rapp and his society."

For want of a full understanding of all the circumstances attending those two cases, it may be objected, that they were not similar,—that Shriver had already commenced an action, which was still pending in the court of Common Pleas,—that the petitioners pointed out no definite mode of relief, &c.—To which we reply, that including these circumstances, the cases appear perfectly similar. It is well known that a suit was instituted by the party, nearly a year ago, which is yet pending. The defendants having obtained a change of venue, it was moved from Mercer county to Anderson, and there tried, at the last November Term, but the jury differing with the judge and counsel, it was suspended for another trial, and yet remains in suspense. As for the mode of relief dictated to our legislature we can conceive nothing in it beyond what was suggested in Shriver's complaint. "He also sets forth (says the report) that numbers through ignorance have been drawn into the slavery of George Rapp through the delusion of being joint partners of the institution, &c." By recourse to the Watch Tower of July 7, 1827, complaints of delusion perfectly similar, on the part of our opponents, may be seen in full detail, equally implying that they thought themselves copartners of the institution. "It is true (say they) we contemplate legislative interference, in reference to the mode and manner of suit against the society, by the adoption of a remedy commensurate to the existing rights of the withdrawing member, which we flatter ourselves can be done without a stretch of legislative power; and this is deemed necessary in consequence of the numbers of the society, say three or four hundred, their peculiar internal regulations that serves to embarrass a direct approach of them by suit, and a speedy judicial decision upon the points in controversy between us."

The learned amanuensis plainly shows that he was equally under the same delusion, in supposing the whole community actually confederated on the principles of a copartnership; and so far carried the delusion into the legislature as to stretch their power into a confirmation of it, without which no adequate remedy could be hoped for. The question, whether a society having no charter of incorporation, has a legal existence, or can either sue or be sued, was promptly answered (and it appears very justly) in the negative, by the Judiciary Committee, in the case of the Economy Society; which principle, if generally correct, may well be said to embarrass a direct approach by suit of three or four hundred people, situated as we are, and known only by names and descriptions, palmed upon us by the public. The society at Economy and that at Pleasant Hill are equally based on the mutual agreement of members, ratified by their signatures to a written covenant, which covenant commits the one interest, designed for the common benefit, to the entire control of certain responsible individuals, as trusted property, to be disposed of according to statutes well defined. These are "the peculiar internal regulations" that render a stretch of legislative power so necessary; and if the late act can be so construed, as to nullify these internal regulations, and constitute three or four hundred people a joint stock company capable of suing and being sued, we must either be cited to some maxim in law, of which we are wholly ignorant, or draw the irrefragable conclusion, that the foregoing act resulted from a stretch of legislative power, beyond what the legislature of Pennsylvania thought to exist in our national government.

But to determine the main inquiry, recourse must be had to facts relating to the proper form, order and character of the society,—whether it is a civil or religious association, and what are its articles of agreement, laws and customs, under which it may be cognizable or otherwise by the civil institutions of the land. In order to commence these general inquires, we shall first introduce the public statements, deliberately given, by the scribe and principal instigater of the aforesaid petition, willing, that from his own pen, the grounds of complaint and the general character and order of the society may be construed.

Statements of John Whitbey concerning the Society; extracted from his book entitled—A short account of Shakerism.

"As liberty of the press has become a powerful means of disseminating knowledge, many avail themselves of its wonderful advantages in communicating their thoughts, views and experience to their fellow creatures. And if I, as a free citizen of the American republick, claim this right, it is with no other than an honest intention of communicating my own just, impartial and candid views of a virtuous people, who have long been the object of idle speculation to some, and of serious reflection, wonder and astonishment to others.

"This people is that society known by the name of *Shakers.* A people with whom I once lived in that degree of union and comfortable feelings which language cannot express nor pen describe; and a people for whom I still feel a kind and tender respect.

"Many are the strange views, false notions and erroneous ideas existing in the minds of strangers concerning that society, and many are the ill-founded conjectures and mistaken opinions of the nature of their system and their principle of government.—They are, in fact, so completely secluded from the world in all their ways, that it is impossible for strangers to form a correct idea of that principle of government or uniting tie that holds them together. It will also be a very difficult thing to give to the world, in writing, just and correct views of the principles of their system and the influence of their government:—But as I have been well acquainted with them as a member of their community for more than seven years, I hope by a correct statement of a number of well known facts to make myself understood on the subject, and give satisfaction to many who are anxious to know, by what unknown art, this peculiar people are bound together as a distinct body." p. 3, 4.

"I first became acquainted with the Shakers, at Pleasant Hill, Mercer county, Ky. in the spring of the year 1818. On becoming acquainted with them, I found them very different from what they were generally represented. Instead of that superstitious gloom and religious melancholy which I expected to see—cheerfulness, satisfaction, peace and tranquillity appeared to reign throughout their delightful dominions.—This was shortly after the division of the society into the first and second orders; this separation being made for the comfort and advantage of both parties—that the first might enter into the practice of such rules and orders as might advance them in the spirit of their system, unmolested by the young and inexperienced—and that the second might remain a while longer in their inexperienced state, undisturbed by the galling yoke of such orders as they were not prepared as yet to receive.

"The second or (as it was called) young order, at that time consisted of one small family.—There were several larger families in the first or Church order, under the direction of such elders of their own order as were chosen by the Ministry. The Ministry was composed of three of each sex, who were the founders of that society, and were originally from the East: of these there were two, one of each sex, whom the society called Father and Mother, who stood as a centre of influence to the others; but in all their proceedings in government they were completely united. Being a stranger, I was unable to form a correct idea of the principles of government and practical regulations of their community, but the visible effects of their system were very delightful."—p. 24, 25.

So much for the views of this writer, on his first acquaintance with the society; the following contains the result of his seven years experience and observation relative to the government, order, economy and moral character of each of the different classes or the body collectively.

Government. "Their government is a kind of hierarchial monarchy, the legislative, judicial and executive powers belonging solely to the Priests or Elders. Among these are different degrees of authority, according to their respective offices, rising in gradation from the lowest to the highest or supreme power.

Each society is divided into families, commonly dwelling in large and convenient houses.—There are in every well organized family two of each sex called elders, who stand as general directors or instructers to the family in every respect, but more especially in all their moral economy; they are also assisted by one or more of each sex called deacon and deaconess, whose business it is to superintend all the domestic [or temporal] concerns of the family, according to their instructions from the elders.—And as every private member is under the direction of his respective deacon, the deacon under the elders, and the elders under the ministry, they are enabled by that means to preserve a strict uniformity and correct understanding of all general affairs throughout the whole society. The interest of all the members in each distinct order of the society is one (according to the practice of the first christians.)" p. 5.

"After coming into Church order, they live in one united interest, altogether under the control of the ministry, elders, trustees and deacons; securing all their previously acquired wealth to the exclusive use of the church by signing a contract or form of covenant to that amount. The case is something different before entering into church order; for when any person first joins the society, an inventory is made of the amount of his property, and if he leave the society before he sign the church covenant, his pro-

petty or the amount of it is restored; but compensation for labour is seldom made." p. 20.

Distinction of Classes. "Almost every society is divided into classes or orders, according to their experience; those who have been gathered together for some years, and have gained a reconciliation and love to their manner of life, are separated from the new beginners; as this class is not prepared, by previous habits, to yield that obedience to good order as is required of the older members. After the commencement of a new society, it requires several years' training of the members to prepare them for what is called *Church* order; but what this order is, I am not able to explain in every respect, having never resided therein; yet I think their rules are similar to those prescribed for the younger class, though far more strict and numerous." p. 11, 12.

Moral Rules. "The instructions, or rather requisitions of the elders not only embrace the general outlines and principles of action, but descend to the more *minute* or *details* of practice, comprehending their whole economy. These orders certainly contain a collection of the best and purest of morals, including the whole duty of man, and are not excelled by any people on earth." p. 13.

"They are a people of excellent morals, very industrious, and in cleanliness, decency, temperance and good order unequalled; and as a body, remarkably kind and benevolent; commonly speaking and acting towards each other in the most respectful manner. And though they are a people of deep humility, keen sensibility and modest deportment, yet they are cheerful, affable and uncommonly social." p. 5.

"Every one has his own peculiar place or office assigned him, not only in occupation, but in meeting, at table and in all other respects; the whole presenting a delightful scene of good order and uniformity." p. 19.

Spirit of Government. "Although the powers of government belong solely to the priests, they generally govern in the mildest manner possible.—The elders often meet with great difficulty in training and bringing beginners into proper order. Some are lazy—some are fractious—some are stubborn, &c. &c. These tumultuous scenes of imperfection and counteraction are generally borne by the elders with great patience; but not without the utmost exertions, in the exercise of such means, as they consider best calculated to bring each one into proper order; exhorting them to depend entirely on the gift of God for that power which will subdue all the evils of a depraved mind, and enable them to gain that purity, love and union, in the spirit of holiness that will consummate their happiness. This manner of conduct becomes a powerful incentive to good order; for all must acknowledge, that the orders and requisitions of the elders are generally founded in strict propriety." p. 15. "Thus, by the influence of the elders, and their assistance to each other, they advance from one degree to another, becoming more and more reconciled to their manner of life, as habit renders it agreeable, and better and better prepared to receive and practise more orderly rules. Having cut themselves off from nearly all sociability, friendship and communications with the world, by renouncing its practices, they have no other source of social enjoyment, than the exercise of kind feelings, union and love among themselves; and to this they gradually attain, to a degree (I believe) exceeded by no society on earth."—p. 17.

Moral Virtue. "The common idea among strangers, that the Shakers live in fornication, adultery and debauchery is too absurd and ridiculous, and betrays such ignorance of the nature of their system, that I think it unworthy of notice. The same may be said of their *bondage* and *slavery* so much spoken of; as though people of common sense would suffer themselves to be bound in a free country contrary to their own choice." p. 20.—" Almost every thing favourable may be said of the Shakers, respecting their moral virtues, the practice of which is productive of great peace, comfort and tranquillity." p. 21.—" Although the Shakers are a misrepresented and persecuted people, I well know they hold a superior place among the various societies of the world in practical virtue."

Temporal Living. "Their co-operative industry produces the comforts of animal life in abundance, and they excel any people with whom I have been acquainted in the art of cookery. But as they are by no means satisfied with a mere negative virtue, or the bare removal of the causes of animal sufferings, their greatest exertions are directed to that cultivation of intellect and *purification* of mind which will raise them to the highest state of mental enjoyment."—p. 21.

Religious Tenets. "The shakers have made several publications of their own faith, ably supported according to their peculiar manner of reasoning." p. 5.—"They believe that the Scriptures were written by inspiration;—They believe, that salvation from sin and redemption from misery are to be gained, through and by Christ.—They have no faith in the resurrection of the animal body after death, but they consider the *soul* the proper subject of the resurrection. Neither do they eat *bread* and drink *wine* in commemoration of an *absent* Christ, for they declare that Christ has returned, and has taken up his abode in and with them, and of course, is always *present*. As they believe that the forbidden fruit which caused the fall and depravity of man is the *flesh*, they of course believe that it is impossible for any one to be saved from the effects of the fall while living in the flesh. And as they believe that the forgiveness of sins belongs to God in Christ, and in Christ alone, and as Christ, on earth, is no where to be found but in his own church—they think it highly necessary, that all who become members of their community, should honestly confess all their sins to God in his living temple, [the priests] receive forgiveness, and be prepared thereby to enter on the work of regeneration."—p. 6 to 12.

The sum of the foregoing statements (which in the main are admitted as correct) is, that the Society in this place was originally founded by a Ministry from the east, two of whom the society called Father and Mother. That the government introduced was, confessedly, a theocracy or divine government, in which the parentage was first in point of authority and ministerial influence: That Trustees, Elders, and Deacons were appointed to various lots of care, spiritual and temporal. That after the example of the primitive christian church, all that believed came together, disposed of their property, and were confederated and united in one interest, in all things. That the consecration of the property, thus united, was to pious and charitable purposes, and that proper persons were authorised, by mutual agreement, to exercise control over it as trusted property, to be appropriated to the use and benefit of the church. That many years' training is deemed necessary to prepare for entering into such an order. That the grand object of the society is, the promotion of virtue, goodness and mutual happiness. That their rules are founded in strict propriety, and are conducive to peace, love and harmony. That, in a temporal sense, they live well—are industrious, neat and cleanly. That they believe the Scriptures—believe in Christ —in the resurrection—confession of sin—regeneration and other christian doctrines, &c. Now what is there, in all this, so essentially variant in point of form, from other religious communities, or charitable institutions, that it should be declared lawful to prosecute suits, &c. against this particular society, in a manner distinct from all others? Are not the official characters, authorised to make and fulfil contracts sufficiently plain and manifest? No individual is admitted into membership with the society, but in agreement with the spiritual lead; nor is any contract made or implied, relating to property, otherwise than with an agent, or some individual, personally responsible for the same, and against whom an action could be brought, provided the case was, in itself, actionable. But as the author of the foregoing statements was but a catechumen, admitted, at an advanced period, into the junior class, and never initiated into church order, it will be proper, for the more perfect understanding of all things from the beginning, to give a circumstantial detail of facts, founded on the certain knowledge and experience of those who have been members of the society, from its early commencement to the present date.

The origin and progress of the United Society at Pleasant Hill.

It is sufficiently manifest, in all our publick writings, that the people known by the name of Shakers originated from a Testimony opened in Europe about the middle of the last century, and brought over to America, in the year 1774. That, according to said testimony (which is, that Christ has made his second appearance) the church is constituted, in the order it is, and the practical rules and orders thereof adopted, as a bond of union, throughout the different branches of the community, wherever they may be situated. In the year 1805, the *Testimony* was first opened in this part of the country, and received by a few individuals. The year following the number of Believers became considerable, and continued to increase, until the number became sufficient to promise the establishment of a society in the place.

When the poeple began to gather together in a congregated capacity, at this place (now Pleasant Hill) the first thing that was done, by each one, was, to procure and continue a sustenance for himself and family, upon land of his own purchasing, or land rented from the neighbors, according to his choice and ability. Such as purchased land, took the titles in their own names, and each one, himself, was the freeholder of his lands and whole estate, real and personal.

The first germs of unity of interest commenced, in this stage of things, by young persons and others, of both sexes, who were single, coming and residing in those scattered families, and associating with them, for the benefit of religious society and instruction. These agreed, mutually, to labor together, for their common support, in each separate family, without any expectation of other wages. These scattered families, constituting a religious neighbourhood, assembled, statedly, for the purposes of divine worship and the benefit of each other, in their religious experience.

In this stage of things, no difference existed, in the tenures by which they held their property, from the rest of the world. But this was very far short of what was expected by all: accordingly, in a short time, preparations were made to draw into a closer connection, both in respect to things spiritual and temporal; which began by several of the aforesaid families joining together, and residing in one house—selecting such places as were most central and convenient, and leaving some of the places, where they had formerly resided, as vacant and out-tenements.

They now began to assume the form and appearance of a village, and each of these, now large families, cultivated its share of those neighbouring farms, from which they derived a part of their support. This state of things rendered it necessary that some change and order should take place, in the management of their property; but nothing like a dedication of property as yet took place. Each one still retained, as formerly, the fee simple of his own real estate; the personal and perishable property of each individual was valued, article by article, and inventoried, the use of which, together with the rents, issues and profits of the land, was freely devoted to their general family purposes, including their own support. And for the better regulation of the general concern, managers were appointed, to see to the general distribution and disposal of all temporal matters.

During the continuance of this order. any one who thought proper, could withdraw from the society, and receive again the whole of his or her property, on giving the necessary previous notice of such intention. In this way the whole connection could dissolve their relation, at pleasure, and the tenures and titles of their property be in themselves unimpaired, as those of other men. This, however, by no means satisfied the community. It was viewed by the members as being far short of what they had set out for; a full and entire union in all things, in perfect imitation of the primitive gospel church, had, from the beginning, been contemplated; and to this point they progressed, in the manner they did, for the purposes of gaining experience and knowledge, in matters relating to a final and decisive compact. That such a course of deliberation should be adopted, must be viewed, even by the worst enemies of the society, as an evidence of its uprightness and purity of intention; especially when it is considered

3

that this novitiate state was maintained for the term of six or seven years, during which time persons might come and go, at pleasure, carrying with them their property, as their own, without having either incurred debt or sustained loss or damage.

This much being said concerning the society in its preparatory state, for the final adoption of church order, we will now consider the steps taken in constituting the order of the church. After the society became fully satisfied of the practicability of union in all things, having, by long experience, tested its general principles, they determined to enter into an explicit covenant, to establish a permanent foundation, for the support of all who chose to dedicate and devote themselves to that manner of life, independent of the personal claims of individuals.—Agreeing, that each member should now make an irredeemable sacrifice of his personal or private interest, his time and talents, without any possibility, on his part, of even an equity of redemption in future. Accordingly, an article of agreement was prepared, carrying all these important features and provisions, the signing of which was familiarly called by the members, *"finally shutting the door."* This transaction produced an important change, in point of titles to the property, which had formerly been held personally by the members now including the order of the Church. The Church covenant, as it was called, was intended and understood to be a firm obligation for the legal conveyance and actual delivery of all and singular the property and estate real and personal of the individual who signed it; and by the signing of this article, the sole rights, titles and claims, in a legal point of view, were intended to be vested in trustees, who were named in said covenant, to be held by them, in trust, for the use and benefit of this newly constituted body called the Church. And thus the individual titles and claims of members, on the ground of private interest, were forever extinguished, and the whole placed, as trusted property, in the hands of trustees, the execution of whose trust, was directed by the covenant. Accordingly such as held real estate, proceeded without delay, in conformity to the aforesaid covenant, to execute regular deeds of conveyance, by which they set over the entire fee simple of their lands, to the trustees aforesaid; moreover, all goods, chattels, household furniture, and property of every description, specified on the inventories of individuals or otherwise claimed by them, were surrendered, and under the superintendence of the trustees, distributed and apportioned to the different households and individual members as every one had need; while the members respectively entered into their different lots and employments, improving their time and talents for the mutual benefit of all; and so it has continued to the present date.

It is needless to recapitulate the object of those proceedings. It only remains to inquire into their legality and moral honesty. And first, Was the plan of thus constituting the church a legal one? Ans. It is certainly entitled to the free toleration and protection of the law. "No man shall be compelled to attend, erect or support any place of worship, against his consent," but a voluntary contribution to any society cannot be prohibited. Perhaps this inquiry could not receive a better answer than the following extract of a private letter, written by William Plumer, Governor of New Hampshire, and published in the Intelligencer of Lancaster (Pa.) dated Feb. 28, 1818.

"My sentiments on that subject, (Religious Freedom) have not changed with time, but every revolving season has added new proofs in my mind, to the fitness and propriety of leaving every individual to the full and entire liberty of choosing his own religion, and of giving or withholding his property, as he pleases, for its support. Human laws cannot make men religious, but they may and often have made bad men hypocrites. Civil government was instituted for earth, not for heaven, and it ought never to intermeddle with religion, except to protect men in the free enjoyment of their religious sentiments."

Q. But is it consistent with moral honesty, to hold the property of an individual who has thus conveyed it to the use and benefit of the church, after he has withdrawn from the community? A. We deem it perfectly so, nor could any thing be more sacrilegious or dishonest, than for any one to attempt the recovery of property thus solemnly and confidentially devoted, in union with others, to the support of an institution, by which all are generally benefitted.

Q. Provided the withdrawing member has failed in receiving those benefits which he expected. What then? A. The blame is his own; he has to abide the consequence. Q. Would it not consist with moral honesty, at least, to refund the principal, or the amount of what he put in the general fund? A. Not as a debt; because he has no claim, on any just principle, and moreover, by the terms of his covenant, he has put it out of the power of the trustees ever to refund it to him, they being bound to appropriate it to the use and benefit of the church and the poor, and to no personal or private end or purpose whatever. Nevertheless, this does not prevent his receiving any charitable donation which the church may think proper, provided his situation and deportment render him worthy. It never was the design of the church to get away people's property from them, nor is it from any lack of honesty or liberality that any such property is withheld. Every well informed mind must see the path of rectitude in this affair, without any mistake. The contributors to a pious or charitable fund necessarily divest themselves and their heirs, of all private or personal claim to such contributions; but they are not divested of their proper authority, as trustors, to compel an execution of the trust; hence it is repugnant to the plainest principles of both law and equity, for the trustees to dispose of such property, otherwise than as directed by the covenant. It is further inquired, whether the church is not bound in conscience to afford a generous patrimony to the children of withdrawing members. To this we reply, that all, before signing the church covenant, have full liberty to make any reserve of property for their children that they choose. Such reserves are deposited in the church, free from interest, until the heir becomes of age and demands and receives it, otherwise signs the covenant and becomes a member; in which event all private claims relating to such estate are forever extinguished. Therefore as the execution of the trust relating to all such devoted property is restricted to the benefit of the church and the poor, the child of a contributor can have no stronger claims on the property than other persons in similar situations; if it be an object of charity, a gift can be extended, but not otherwise.

Having considered the claims of withdrawing members and their natural heirs, we shall next consider the claims of those members who maintain a good standing and continue to be held in union with the body. But to enter fully into this subject, embracing every important question that might arise, relating to the different lots and offices of members, may not be necessary. It must, however, be observed, that by virtue of the church covenant, a total transfer of all legal title and claim to the property has been made, from each and every member of the church, to certain individuals as agents or trustees, who are bound to use it for the purposes specified above: Hence the only right or claim remaining in individual members, is to their equal and daily dividends of food, clothing and other necessaries, in sickness, health and old age, according to their respective needs. The trustees, also being members, have a right to manage and dispose of it, as directed, so long as they are held in office, and act in union with the body, and no longer. It might be further inquired, whether the trustees do not, some how or other, hold a personal claim, superior to other members. This, by no means, is implied in the covenant. The property of the trustees, real and personal, is as substantially conveyed and consecrated to the benefit of the community, as the property of any other member, and they are equally subject to the same governing influence with others.

It may also be inquired, whether the control and management of this property is so confided to the trustees, that no private member can trade or speculate upon it, under pretence of an individual right? Ans. As to individual right, that point, we presume, has been fully settled; and should individuals assume a right to make any disposal of it, without authority from the trustees, any such contract would be deemed illegal, and property thus perverted recoverable by law, to its proper use and appropriation.

Now from all that has been said, it is easy to infer the falsity and absurdity of the common charge of dishonesty so frequently cast upon the institution. Does it belong to the character of knaves and swindlers to consecrate and devote all they possess to a common use and benefit? If fraud was intended, would the candidate for church membership be allowed seven years probation, and afforded every possible privilege of examining the subject to the bottom before he signs the covenant of consecration? It is truly a matter of deep regret when any one enters into the bonds of the covenant, and proves unfaithful to his solemn obligations; no sacrifice of property on the part of the church could repair the incalculable damages that result from the withdrawal of such. We do not mean in personal abuse or private injuries, but in disseminating false reports and accusations, dishonoring the gospel, sowing discord among neighbours, and disturbing the peace and happiness of society. The nature and obligations of the church covenant are so plainly taught among us, and so well understood by all, that we have no reason to believe, that any one ever attempted to give up and consecrate his property with any expectation of ever receiving it again; nor can any church member have the smallest reason to expect wages for his work when it is so well known, that each individual is his own employer, and receives the services of others as freely as he bestows his own.

We the undersigned, having, at an early period, become members of the United Society, in this place, and as such maintained our standing to the present date, do cheerfully subscribe to the foregoing statement of facts as correct, and the reasons offered in support of them consistent with our faith and the well known principles of the institution.

E. Thomas, J. Voris, J. Runyon, B. Burnett, A. Dunlavy, H. Banta, P. Veris, F. Montfort, S. Manire, J. Vanclave, V. Runyon, M. Burnett, J. Congleton, G. R. Runyon, J. Shields, W. Runyon, A. Fite, M. Thomas, J. Coony, J. L. Ballance, J. Lineback, D. Woodrum, J. Shane, S. Harris, J. Badget, T. Shane, J. Voris, jr. S. Badget, W. Verbrike, J. Medlock, P. Hooser, P. Lineback, W. Manire, G. D. Runyon, L. Wilhite.

It has not been uncommon for individuals to withdraw from the junior order of the society, who rarely make any difficulty in settling their accounts, the terms being so well understood. And although there have also been various instances of members withdrawing from the church, there has never, as yet, been a case in this country, in which the legal force of the church covenant has been tested before a court of justice. In other States it has been somewhat different, as will appear from the following documents.

To the United Society of Believers in Kentucky.

Having understood that your rights as citizens, or the legality of our covenant, is about to be put to the test at a court of law, and that you wish to know how such cases have been decided in Massachusetts, we are able to assure you, that the covenant, as well as our legal rights, has been several times put to the test before the supreme judicial court (or the court of appeals as you call it) and that our society has been declared from this bench to be a legal compact, and our covenant a legal instrument—and that before this court there never has been a decree given against us, nor has it, in any instance, invalidated the legality of our institution—and that having been an eye and ear witness of these transactions for upwards of thirty years, I hereby certify, that I have heard it pronounced by Francis Dana, Chief Justice of said court, that it was as illegal to trespass on our rights, as on those of any other society whatever; and other judges have decided in the same way. We have always faced those unjust and illegal demands or charges with confidence and perseverance, so that we have never lost a case, and our prayer is that the same success may attend you on these occasions, &c.

ASA BROCKLEBANK.

Among the various communications we have received from different quarters affording light on the subject, three cases in particular seem to merit special notice—two containing the opinion of the supreme judicial court in the State of Maine, the other the report of an action tried in the county of Grafton, State of New Hampshire, in 1810, which cases furnish such special light on almost every point that can come into controversy relating to our civil rights, that we think them worthy of a place in the present publication. The first two may be found at large in 3rd and 4th Greenleaf, Reporter for Maine, and the latter in the New Hampshire law case, published in the National Intelligencer of December 1st, 1827.

State of Maine, Alfred, April Term, 1825.
ANDERSON ET AL. vs. BROCK.

In trespass quare clausum by the trustees of the society of Shakers for an injury done to their common property. The members of the same society are competent witnesses on releasing, &c.

This was an action for trespass of breaking the close of the plaintiffs. They sued as deacons or overseers of the society of Shakers, and so amended their writ, which was objected to by the defendant, but sustained by the court. The competency and incompetency of the witnesses were argued at length on both sides. The court decided in favour of their competency.

The plaintiff's counsel then read a deed from Barbara Brown to Gowen Wilson, &c. conveying the *locus in quo* to them and their successors and assigns, in trust for the use of the society, the support of the Gospel among them, &c. and then showed from the book of Records of the society that the plaintiffs were then regular successors,

The defendants contended that no title had passed to the plaintiffs, and therefore they had no right to maintain the action.

The objection was overruled by the court and a verdict under its instructions, was returned for the plaintiffs, subject to the opinion of the Court.

At the succeeding term in Kennebeck, Weston, J. delivered the opinion of the court, in which it holds the doctrine that the trustees of the Shakers have a right to, as such, and can maintain an action against a wrong doer to the common property of the Shakers. The court seems to be under a strong conviction, that the trustees can maintain an action declaring upon their own possession and seisin without setting forth their official character—where a defendant can show no title in himself, he may not rely on the weakness of the trustees' title, and judgment for damages at the suit of the trustees must be rendered against him, declaring upon their own rights.

The doctrine was urged by the counsel for the plaintiff, that where a regular deed of trust was made to the plaintiffs and their successors, so long as the succession was susceptible of proof, the successors would take at common law. *Newhall vs. Wheeler, 7th Mass. Rep. p.* 179.

The court in giving their opinion hold out the following language: "But religious toleration, which is the vital principle of protestantism, and which is effectually secured by the constitution and laws of our own State, as well as that from which we have separated, has produced and is producing many modifications of discipline and doctrine in bodies associated for spiritual and ecclesiastical purposes. The sect with which the plaintiffs are connected have been for some time known among us, and their peculiar tenets and modes of discipline have been embodied and settled by their teachers in regular and, among them, well established forms. Although once persecuted by the mistaken zeal of former days, they are now permitted under more favourable auspices to keep the peaceful tenor of their way unmolested. They are in general quiet, sober and industrious; and the fruits of these commendable qualities are exhibited to the public eye in their beautiful villages and cultivated grounds; and in the apparent comfort and abundance with which they are surrounded. If the persons who acquire authority and influence among them, should be found to abuse these powers, they are answerable both civilly and criminally for their misconduct. Like all other citizens they are amenable to the laws by which they are protected; and from obedience to which their seclusions afford them no immunity or exemption."

After much luminous argument in support of their opinion, the court gave judgment upon the verdict.—See 3d Greenleaf, 243.

WAIT vs. MERRIL AND AL.

Mellen, C. J.

This case presents two questions for consideration. 1. Were John Coffin, Levi Holmes and Elisha Pate properly admitted as witnesses? and 2d, were the instructions of the Judge to the jury correct?

1. The objection to the admission of the above mentioned witnesses seems to have been effectually removed by the releases given at the trial. A question of the same nature was settled by this court, in the case of Anderson and al. vs. Brock, 3 Greenleaf: The only difference is, in *that* case the witnesses were introduced by the plaintiff, and *they* and the witnesses executed mutual releases. This objection therefore is overruled.

2d. The second deserves more consideration. Under the instructions which the jury received, they have found that the plaintiff *knowingly signed the covenant;* and, by the report, it appears that he was a man of common natural abilities and understanding, and sometimes taught and exhorted in the religious meetings of the society; and he was more than twenty one years of age when he signed it. By thus signing, he assented to all the terms and conditions specified in that covenant, made its stipulations his own, and agreed to conform to the rules and regulations of the society in relation to its spiritual and temporal concerns. By the covenant, it appears, and also from the testimony of the plantiff's own witnesses, that *community of interest* is an established and distinguishing principle of the association:—that the services of *each* are contributed for the benefit of *all,* and *all* are bound to maintain *each* in health, sickness and old age, from the common or joint-fund, created and preserved by joint industry and exertion—and each one by the express terms of the covenant, engages "never to bring debt or demand against the said deacons, nor "their successors, nor against any member of the church or com- "munity, jointly or severally on account of any service or pro- "perty, thus devoted and consecrated to the aforesaid sacred and "charitable use."

Such are the facts, as to the contract into which the plaintiff entered, when he subscribed the covenant. It is an *express* contract. The plaintiff, in the present action, however, does not profess to found his claim on an *express* promise; but he contends that upon the facts proved, and disclosed in the report before us, the law *implies a promise* on the part of the defendants, to pay him for his services, although they were performed for the *society* of which the defendants are officers, and not for them in their private capacity; and although such an *implied promise* is directly repugnant to the covenant or *written contract.* Besides it is clear, from all the evidence in the cause, that whatever services the plaintiff performed while he was a member of the society, and remained and labored with them, he performed in consequence of his membership and in pursuance of the covenant, and in virtue of which he became a member. Now it is a principle perfectly well settled, that where there is an *express* contract in force, the law does not recognize an *implied* one, and where services have been performed under an *express* contract, the action to recover compensation for such services must be founded on *that* contract, and on *that only*, unless in consequence of the *fault* or *consent* of the defendant. In the present case there is no proof that the covenant has been violated on the part of the society, or that the plaintiff had any right to *waive* the covenant and its special provisions, and resort to a supposed implied promise, on which to maintain his action. But as the covenant refers to the *order* of the church and their peculiarities of faith, and as at the trial both parties, without objection, went into an examination of witnesses, and thus obtained all those facts, in relation to the society which are detailed in the judge's report, the argument of the counsel has been founded on *all the evidence* in the cause, received in a body; and, of course, in forming our opinion we shall place it on the same broad foundation, without reference to technical objections if any should present themselves. We are perfectly satisfied, that the covenant was properly admitted as proof to the jury, to show on what terms and considerations, the services were performed by the plaintiff, for which he is now seeking compensation. We are also of opinion that the instructions of the judge to the jury were correct, if the covenant signed by the plaintiff, taken in connection with those facts in the cause which are considered on this occasion as a part of it, is a *lawful covenant*, one which the law will sanction, as not being inconsistent with *constitutional rights, moral precepts or public policy.* This leads us to the examination of the covenant, the principles it contains and enforces, and the duties it requires of the members of the society. The counsel for the plaintiff contends that the covenant is, for certain reasons, *void*, and to be pronounced by this court a *nullity*. It is said that it is void, because it deprived the plaintiff of the constitutional powers of *acquiring, possessing and protecting property*. The answer to this objection is, that the covenant only *changed* the *mode* in which he chose to exercise this right or power. He preferred that the avails of his industry should be placed in the common fund or bank of the society and to derive his maintenance from the daily dividends which he was sure to receive. If this is a valid objection, it certainly furnishes a new argument against Banks, and is applicable also to partnerships of one description as well as another. It is said that the covenant or contract is contrary to the *genius* and *principles* of a *free government* and therefore void. To this it may be replied, that one of the blessings of a *free government* is, that under its mild influences the citizens are at liberty to pursue that mode of life and species of employment best suited to their inclinations and habits, unembarrassed by too much regulation; and while thus peaceably occupied, and without interfering with the rights or enjoyments of others, they surely are entitled to the protection of so good a government as ours; then, perhaps *all these* privileges and enjoyments might be contrary to the genius and principles of an *arbitrary* government. But in support of this objection, it is contended that the covenant is a contract on perpetual service and surrender of liberty. Without pausing to inquire whether a man may not legally contract with another to serve him for *ten* years as well as one, receiving an acceptable compensation for his services, we would observe that by the very terms of the fourth and fifth articles, a *secession* of members from the society is contemplated, and its consequences guarded against in the fifth, by the covenantors never to make any claim for their services, against the society; and the fourth article speaks of a compliance with certain rules, so long as they "remained in obedience to the order and government of the church, and holden in relation as members." Besides, the general understanding and usage for persons to leave the society whenever they incline so to do, the plaintiff himself has, in this case, given us proof of this right, by withdrawing from their fellowship; and now, in the character of a stranger to their rules and regulations, demanding damages in consequence of the dissolution of his contract.

It is said the covenant is void, because it is in derogation of the *inalienable right of liberty of conscience*. To this objection the reply is obvious. The very formation and subscription of the covenant is an exercise of the inalienable right of liberty of conscience; and it is not easy to discern why the society in question may not frame their creed and covenant as well as other societies of christians, and worship God according to the dictates of their own consciences. We must remember that in this land of liberty, civil and religious, conscience is subject to no human law; its rights are not to be invaded or even questioned, so long as its dictates are obeyed consistently with the harmony, good order and peace of the community. With us modes of faith and worship must always be numerous and variant, and it is not the province of either branch of the government to control or restrain them, when they appear sincere and harmless. Again, it is urged that the *covenant* is void, because its consideration is illegal, that it is against *good morals* and the *policy of the law*. We apprehend that these objections cannot have any foundation in the covenant itself, for that is silent as to many particulars and peculiarities which the counsel for the plaintiff deems objectionable. The covenant only settles certain principles as to the admission of members; community of interest; mode of management and support; requisition and use of the property; stipulations in respect to services and claims; professions of a *general nature*, as to the faith of the society, and the solemn renewal of a former covenant and appointment of certain officers. This is the essence of the covenant signed by the plaintiff, and on this the defendants rely as a *written contract* of the plaintiff under his hand and seal, never to make the present claim, and also a complete bar to it. Now what is there illegal in its consideration, or wherein is it against *good morals* and the *policy of the law?* It *does not* contain a *fact* or a *principle* which an honest man ought to condemn; but it *does* contain some provisions which all men ought to approve. It distinctly inculcates the duty of honest industry, contentment with competency, and charity to the poor and suffering.

In *this* view of the subject these objections vanish in a moment. But if we consider them as founded on the *covenant* and *all the evidence in the cause together,* the result of the examination, will not, in a *legal* point of view, be essentially varied. It is certainly true, that some articles of faith, peculiar to the society, appear to the rest of the world as destitute of all scriptural foundation, and several of their consequent regulations unnatural, whimsical, and in their tendency in some respects, calculated to *weaken* the force of what are termed *imperfect obligations.* Professing to exercise a most perfect command over those passions which *others* are disposed most cheerfully to *obey;* they, perhaps, in so doing may chill some of the kindest affections of the heart, gradually lessen its sensibility, and to a certain extent, endanger, if not seriously wound, "the tender charities of father, son and brother." Perhaps celibacy, out of the pale of this church, has often the same tendency. It is true, the mode of education and government may be too restrictive, and the means used to preserve proper submission to authority may be deemed artful, severe, and in some particulars highly reprehensible, especially in their pretended knowledge of the secrets of the heart. On the other hand, it appears as before stated, that benevolence and charity are virtues enjoined and practised, and the plaintiff's witnesses, who had formerly belonged to the society for several years, testified, that " all vice and immorality are disallowed in the society, and integri-
" ty, uprightness and purity of life are taught and enforced among
" them; and that the precepts of the gospel, as they understand
" and interpret them, constitute, as they conceive, the foundation
" of their faith, and the rules of their practice." As for their *faith,* it would seem, from the volumes which they have published, that it extends to unusual lengths, and leads to what others at once pronounce to be absurdities; but this is not within our controul; it is rightfully their own.

But it is contended, that, according to the faith and principles, and usages of the society, which are considered as referred to, in the covenant as a part of it, the covenant amounts to a contract never to *marry,* which *public policy* will not sanction. We have before observed that it is not a *perpetual one,* of course, *at most,* it is a contract not to marry while they continue members of the society; but their faith does not require *so much* as this, their principles condemn marriage in certain cases only; that is, where it is contracted with carnal motives, and not *purely* with a view of complying with the original command "increase and multiply."

"Tis true they do not believe that marriage is contracted, except in some solitary instances, without motives far less worthy and disinterested. As it regards those members of the society who are married, though they may live separate without cherishing the gentle affections, still such conduct violates no human law; and however lightly they may esteem the blessing of matrimony, their *opinions* do not lessen the *legal* obligations created by marriage. Surely they may agree to live in different houses and without any communication with each other. Contracts of separation between husband and wife are not unfrequent, neither are they *illegal* when made with *third persons*. This objection cannot avail, nor that which refers to the relation between father and son. Their principles require the circle of benevolence and affection to be enlarged, but not that parental or filial tenderness should be destroyed or lessened. We must not overlook the distinction between duties of *perfect* and *imperfect* obligation; the neglect of the former is a violation of law, which will render the delinquent liable in a court of justice to damages, penalties or punishment, but the performance of the latter is never the subject of *legal coercion*. A man may be punished for defrauding his neighbour; but not for indulging feelings of unkindness towards him; or in the hour of sorrow *withholding from him* the balm of sympathy, consolation and relief. Though we may disapprove of many of the *sentiments* of this society in respect to the subject of education and discipline; yet as they steadily inculcate purity of morals, such a society has a perfect right to claim and receive, and enjoy the full blessings of legal protection.

But for the sake of the argument, let us suppose that the contract or covenant is *illegal* and *void*, for the reasons which have been urged by the plaintiff's counsel: what, then, will be the legal consequences? Will the action, then, stand on any firmer ground? Though in the present case, the plaintiff does not demand of the defendants, the re-payment of a sum of money paid to them, on the ground that they have no legal right to retain it, yet his demand is, in principle, the same thing; it is a demand of compensation for services rendered, on the ground, that as the contract was unlawful and void, the value of those services may be recovered: that is, if he had increased the funds of the society by a *sum of money* instead of his *personal labors*, and *services*, the right to *recover back the money*, or recover the *value of those services in money*, must be settled by the *same* principles of law in *both* cases. Now what are those principles? Before stating them, let it be again observed, that the jury have found, that the plaintiff knowingly signed this covenant, which we are now considering in the light of an *illegal* and *void* contract, and voluntarily joined the society and remained several years a member, engaged with all the other members in all the transactions of it, and all of them *in pari delicto;* for if the covenant is illegal and void, it is

4

because the society who formed and signed it is an *unlawful society*, and united for purposes which the law condemns.

'If a wager be made on a boxing match, and on the event happening, the winner receives the money; it cannot be recovered back by the loser, for where one knowingly pays money upon a contract executed which is in itself *immoral and illegal*, and where the parties are *equally* criminal, the rule is, in pari delicto, potior est conditio defendentis.' 2 Com. Con. 120. Bull. n. p. 132, Cowp. 179. Lord Kenyon there says, 'There is no case to be found where, when money has been actually paid by *one* of two parties to the *other*, on an *illegal contract*, both being par*ticeps criminis*, an action can be maintained to recover it back again. Here the money was not paid on an *immoral* though *illegal* consideration; and though the law would not have *enforced* the payment of it, yet, as having paid, it is not against conscience for the defendant to retain it.' Lawrence J. adds "In Smith v. Bromley, Lord Mansfield said, that when *both* parties are equally criminal against the *general laws of public policy* the rule is *potior est conditio defendentis*, better is the condition of the defendant." See Smith v. Bromley, Douglas 696. See, also, Engar and al. v. Fowler 3. Esp. 222, it was determined that an underwriter could not maintain an action against brokers to recover premiums of reassurances declared illegal by statute. Lord Ellenboro' C. J. says, "We will not assist an *illegal transaction* in any respect: we leave matters as we find them, and so an action will not lie to recover back money deposited for the purpose of being paid to one for his interest, and soliciting a pardon for a person under sentence of death."—3 Esp. 253.

"No implied promise rises out of an *illegal transaction*," Robertson v. Tyler, 2 H. Bl. 37 9. See also Aubert v. Moor, 2 Bos. and Pul. 371. And McDane in his abr. 1 vol. 194, says, " And on the whole, the sound principle is, the law will not raise or imply any promise *in aid of* a transaction *forbidden by the law of the land.*" With these authorities it would seem impossible for us to sustain the present action, even allowing the *covenant* and the *society*, by whom and for whose use it was formed, to be of the reprehensible and illegal character which has been given them. On the whole, we are all of opinion there is a total failure on the part of the plaintiff; and accordingly there must be judgment on the verdict.

State of Maine, County of York, Alfred, June 18, 1827.

The above is the opinion of the Supreme J. Court in the State of Maine, delivered at Portland, in the County of Cumberland, in May, 1826, and will be reported in the next volume of Greenleaf's reports, not yet published.

DANIEL GOODENOW,
Counsellor at Law in said Court.

State of New Hampshire, Sup. Court, Grafton County, October Term, 1810.

JOHN HEATH vs. NATHANIEL DRAPER.

Assumpsit for $1000 money had and received, &c. and 2d count for labor and service, per account annexed to writ for 13 years and 11 months—on quantum meruit; amount $2016. Labor ended 17th August, 1809—alleged to have been performed at defendant's request and for his benefit. Plea, non assumpsit.

It was admitted that defendant was a deacon, and had the charge of the temporal concerns of the family of Shakers at Enfield in this State; and that the plaintiff's father, Jacob Heath, and his mother, with their children, joined the society in 1784. The plaintiff was then about 14 years old. The father never was a member of the church, but of the society only.

The plaintiff in 1793—5, after he became of age, joined the church, and signed the covenant. After that time, the father put what he considered as the plaintiff's share of his estate into the hands of the *then* deacons of the society. 8th December, 1798, the deacons (defendant and Lyon) paid the amount to the plaintiff, $175. Plaintiff then returned the money to the deacons, agreeably to the covenant he had entered into with the church in 1793. 26th October, 1801, plaintiff renewed the covenant, as did the other members of the church with some small additions.

It was admitted that the plaintiff had labored faithfully in and for the society, from the time mentioned in the writ, till he withdrew in 1809; and had been clothed and supported out of the joint stock, as others were.

On the part of the plaintiff several witnesses were examined before the jury. The object seemed to be, to prove that the principles and practice of the society were narrow, exclusive, strict, and severe—unfriendly to learning, having little regard to natural ties, and domestic relations;—that professing equality in the members, they were governed by a few, and held to the doctrine of passive obedience, and non resistance, contrary to the constitution.

The defendant gave in evidence the covenant, as it was called, and the renewal of it by plaintiff. The execution was admitted. It was substantially the same as that stated in the book called "The testimony of Christ's second appearing, &c. p. 505, chapter xiii." They also called several witnesses, who gave a more favourable account of the principles and practice of the society, than that given by plaintiff's witnesses—all agreeing that no coercion was used,—members may go away from the church when they please; but in such case, it has always been considered, they have no claim to the property *given,* and dedicated by them, nor to maintenance *in future.* In such cases the church has, on some occasions given them such sums as they thought proper, but nothing as debt or matter of right.

Admission into the church is treated as a matter of solemn consideration—not done hastily, but on full deliberation, and not while the party is under age. No persuasions are used, much less any misrepresentations, as to terms, principles, consequences, &c. All is set down in writing. Steady, but moderate labor is required, according to the ability of the party. The government and discipline of the society is mild and gentle.

The counsel for the defendant gave an historical account of the society from its origin, a short summary of the doctrines and principles of the sect: in substance, the same as stated in the book called "The Testimony of Christ's second appearing," &c. 2d edition printed at Albany 1810; from which he read various passages. The testimony was not summed up by the counsel on either side; it was thought unnecessary. Defendant's counsel briefly stated the grounds on which, in point of law, a recovery was resisted—That here was no *implied* promise to pay wages, but an express agreement that plaintiff was *not laboring* for *hire* or wages: and as to the money put into the joint stock by the plaintiff it was *given*, the gift was *complete and effectual*—possession delivered:—it was not in the power of the donor to retract or reclaim it: that there was no consideration; if such were in fact the case, would only show that it was a gift,—when there is a consideration it is a *grant*. By our law the owner may freely *give* his property, or he may make a worse use of it—if he so please—waste it in riotous living. He may surely bestow his money and labour in support of charity, and what he thinks religion.

Some suppose a donor has an equity to recover back a gift; but the rule is the same in equity as at law—no bill lies—the party merely has the right to ask for a gift in return. It is admitted, that to make the gift effectual and binding, the donor must *give freely*, understanding what he is about—must be under no legal incapacity, such as infancy, coverture, insanity, duresse:—there must be no circumvention or fraud practised upon him: On these points defendant cheerfully submits the cause, on the evidence before the jury. Even plaintiff's testimony does not so much as tend to prove any such things. As to the labor, it was not done for defendant or at his request; but he is willing to waive all objections to *form* and indeed to substance as it respects this point. He is willing the case should be considered in the same way as if the whole of this church or the society were the defendants on the record. Here was no labor done *for the society*, under an expectation of wages, but the contrary. Labor gratuitously performed gives no cause of action any more than a gift of money or other thing. To make a contract there must be an agreement—*aggregatio mentium*: an agreement of both parties, that plaintiff was laboring *for hire*, to be paid by defendants.

The circumstances of the case exclude all implication of contract: *The promise implied by law* is a metaphysical notion—the law in truth *makes* no promise; it is the parties that make *all the contract.* When A says to B labor for me, it is the understanding of both, where the contrary is not expressed, that he is to be paid a reasonable sum, or adequate compensation, where no particular sum is named.

Implied contracts or promises exist only where there is no express stipulation between the parties. Here there was an express stipulation, that plaintiff was *not to be paid.* It is a matter of *faith* with this sect not to claim any thing for property bestowed or services done to their community. Each freely gives, and in their belief is bound to give his time and talents, as brethren and sisters for the mutual good, one of another. This action is a breach of faith as well as of contract. When plaintiff agreed to dedicate his property and his services to this society, he did not suppose he was giving beyond what he received. He was admitted a member and entitled to all the privileges annexed to membership. The consideration has not failed through any cause out of himself. He made a contract—defendants have performed and are ready to perform. Plaintiff alone is dissatisfied and wishes to be off on a new contract of his own making. He has proved himself not so good a man as he professed and they believed him to be. But they are willing still to use their endeavors to reclaim and reform him.

His right in this action to recover is much the same as that of a wife would be, after she had committed adultery and absconded from her husband's family. There might in this case be an equity in plaintiff, if he had been ill used by defendant or the family, and so, as it were, driven away; but the evidence gives no colour for this. Going away was his own voluntary act. If he acted under a mistake of fact or law, in joining the society and entering into the covenant, it would be a different thing, but the evidence negatives any such pretence.

It has been hinted, and *only* hinted, that this dedication of property and labour was to superstitious uses, to a false religion and so not binding. No one can see the improvements made in husbandry and manufactures by this sect, and at the same time believe the existence of the sect to be against the policy of the law. Whatever we may think of their faith, their works are good, and charity bids us think well of the tree when the fruits are salutary. We cannot try the question which religion, theirs or ours, is the better one—Each may prefer his own. Theirs is equally under the protection of the law, as ours. To try this question it would be but fair to empannel a jury de medietate. Suppose this small sect had a court, and our religion, opinions and practice should come on trial before it, what should we think of the correctness of a verdict finding our religion an absurd one and tending to immorality? In matters of faith we are incompetent to judge each other. There certainly are some reasons for saying that the religion of this sect of christians, bears a greater resemblance to that of the primitive church than ours does. Their discipline is more strict, perhaps, than ours, but not more so than that of the first churches of New England, the Presbyterian church of Scotland in former days, or the Methodists a short time ago.

Chief Justice Livermore, (Evans and Steele, Justices, agreeing) summed up in favour of defendant, on the grounds stated above, and the jury found accordingly.

W. H. Woodward and D. Webster for plaintiff.
B. J. Gilbert and J. Smith for defendant.

To the foregoing may be added, the following remarks, in the instructions of the judge to the jury, in the case of Wait vs. Merril, in the court below. After making some remarks on the bitter spirit of prejudice that was in circulation, against the Shakers, he cited them to look back on former ages, and see how many innocent people had suffered for the free exercise of faith and conscience. "We will (said he) only go back to the time when christianity was first introduced into the world, by that, then, despised man, Jesus Christ. There were, then, a few, who separated themselves from the common course of the world; these were despised, and all manner of evil spoken of them—treated with the greatest cruelty, by professor and profane. Now all we who profess the christian faith, are obliged to acknowledge, that they were the people of God.

"Now I warn you to beware what you do against these people called Shakers. God forbid that I should raise my hand or voice against them, as it respects their institution and doctrine of celibacy of which you complain; for it has been proved before us to-day from the highest authority on earth, that the doctrine of celibacy and community of goods, are agreeable to the precepts and example of Christ and the primitive Church.

"This people is not to be crushed: I am not placed on this bench to judge people's consciences, but to see that they are kept free. If any person goes to live with that society, under a profession of their faith, if they never sign any covenant, they cannot recover wages, nor is it right they should. If you let prejudice rule and give this cause against the defendant, it will not avail"—

Upon a review of the foregoing matter, it would seem, that every thing worthy of being called an objection against the order, government and economy of the United Society, has been fully obviated. However, should any professor of either law or gospel, in a spirit of candor, point out any thing illegal or immoral, in the view that has been given of the institution, the society stands ready and willing to pursue the investigation, till reasonable satisfaction is rendered to the candid public: but should persons who acknowledge no test of truth but their own fancy, light up their lanthern of criticism, to shed a false light on any thing that has been stated, no attention from the society need be expected. Any thing flowing from malice or self interest, will be treated as charity and forbearance may dictate.

Our object has not been to stimulate but to administer a sedative to the passions of a selfish nature : not, indeed, to protract, but to bring to a rational decision, a disagreeable contest : for this reason we have avoided as much as possible, any controversy on those *moral sentiments*, so highly applauded by our opponents. We are willing that the converts to those sentiments should enjoy their *mental liberty*, only not try to force their sentiments or themselves into an unnatural association with our sentiments and our Society.

That the celebrated compiler of those newly arranged sentiments selected many good ideas from our Testimony, relative to community principles, needs no other proof than his pamphlet on that subject published in England, and presented to the king and parliament : His candor towards our society, manifested in that work, merits respect; but his taking our wine to mix with his water-lays us under no obligation to mix his water with our wine, seeing the source from which his water is drawn, is so generally disgusting to civil and religious society, and especially so infatuating to some, who, from certain circumstances, have adopted our name and profession.

With regard to the names subscribed to some of the foregoing articles, they imply nothing more than a simple attestation of facts and not a formal defence, on the principle of joint tenancy; which, according to law, would require the names of the whole society to be inserted. There are many at Pleasant Hill, whose names are not written in this book, who stand equally ready to give testimony to the truth, and "justify the way of God to man."

Extract from Dr. Holley's Review of Professor Silliman's Journal. Western Review, vol. 3, p. 203.

"The account of the Shakers near New Lebanon in New-York, is written, in the main, with a benevolent and an apologetical spirit. We were however sorry to see the word 'blasphemous' applied, by so intelligent a casuist as our author, even with the softening note of interrogation that accompanies it. The essence of blasphemy is in the intention, in the state of the mind; and Mr. Silliman can have no design to deny the reality of a sincere Shaker's piety when he is singing his sacred songs.—The writer does not appear to us to have read the large work, called 'Christ's Second Appearing,' or 'Dunlavy's Manifesto,' an octavo volume, when he says in reference to the Shakers, 'They rarely publish any thing respecting their own principles and habits." They have, in fact, given very full statements of their principles, and have laboured, like other believers, to fortify their creed, by numerous quotations from the Bible, and even by criticisms on the Hebrew and Greek originals. They do not differ so much, as is supposed, from the other followers of Christ, when we go beyond their *exoterical* faith, and enter fully into the *esoterical*. Their Christ is, the redeeming, anointing, and consecrating operation of the spirit of God upon human nature, and is not limited to either sex, nor to any age or country. They believe that the Divine Being imparts this blessing, in greater or less degrees, to all the truly religious; and they worship Christ, apparently with great sincerity and zeal, wherever they find satisfactory manifestations of the Divine Gift or Operation. They do not consider the sex affecting this question, nor do they attempt or wish to justify any of the acknowledged errors or sins of Ann Lee. While she was without the anointing grace of God, she was like other persons in the flesh, and served the world in the same manner. Her marriage, and her children only prove, that she was once the property of

Antichrist, but afterwards she was turned to God, and received the First Gift granted, during her life, to any individual on earth. The Divine Spirit is not contaminated by taking any portion of human nature, which it may select, into union with itself. Even unregenerate persons may be used by God as instruments to accomplish his purposes, to convey his truth, to work miracles, to utter prophecies, and to show his power. Those, who were once wicked, may be sanctified, and may furnish a fit residence for a heavenly guest. Ann Lee was thus hallowed and honored. She is called *Mother*, not merely because she was a woman, but because she had the First Gift of the Holy Spirit at the time, and because the Holy Spirit, in its sanctifying influences, as distinguished from the creative or productive power of God the Father, is considered as maternal, as sustaining a character analogous to that of the Mother of the faithful. Properly speaking, God as creator is our Father, but as sanctifier and cherisher, is our mother. The Shakers do not appear to believe that God is actually and literally male and female, but that he has the affections and performs the offices both of Father and Mother in regard to his children. Jesus, being a male, and united to God, was a son, while Ann, being a female, and enjoying a similar union, was a daughter. Jesus however, when considered in relation to his disciples whom he has spiritually begotten in his church, may be denominated Father, as Ann, when considered in relation to her disciples, whom she has brought forth in her church, may be denominated Mother. The highest sense, in which a Shaker uses Father, carries him to God as creator, while the highest sense, in which he uses Mother, carries him to God as sanctifier. It is not our duty to defend these ideas and distinctions, but to state them as an article of justice, towards the singular people, to whom they relate. Mr. Silliman seems not to have been perfectly initiated into the osoteric of their faith.

Another point in their creed, which it is somewhat interesting to know, is this, that New Lebanon in New-York is destined to be always the Metropolitan See, and its church the Vatican of Shakerism. The head or Pope, the individual or individuals having the First Gift on earth, enjoying the most intimate union with God, and appointed to give infallible directions to the people of the true faith, must always reside at New Lebanon. This person, when the Gift falls upon one, may be either male or female; when the Gift falls jointly and equally on two, as it may, and they are of different sexes, they are then the Father and Mother of believers. The common idea, that there is always an Elect Lady, who is the lawful successor of Ann Lee, is erroneous. It happens at this time that Lucy Wright of New-Lebanon is the Elect Lady, or has, as it may be otherwise expressed, the First Gift. But where the Gift is bestowed jointly and equally upon a male and a female, and the female should die first, the male would then be the Elect, and the will of Christ would be made known, by way of eminence, through him. Christ may be called *it*, as well as *he*, or *she;* and it depends on the circumstances of the particular application of the term, whether one of these pronouns, or another, shall be used. When the reference is to Jesus, it is proper to use the pronoun *he* for Christ; when to Ann, the pronoun *she;* and when to the operation of the Holy Spirit, without including any individual person as the instrument, the pronoun *it*.

We do not suppose it to be necessary for us as reviewers to go into further details upon this mystical subject. We only wish to furnish a clue to carry such of our readers through this theological labyrinth as may desire to gratify their curiosity in so great an extent. No faith is more easily misunderstood and misrepresented than that of the Shakers. The metaphysical explanation of it is so different from popular apprehension, that great pains, and some talent in conducting a moral analysis, are necessary to do justice to this remarkable sect. We may be in an error in what we have said, but we have given our impressions fairly, after having read their books and talked much with their teachers. We might easily go on to show that the doctrine of the Trinity is considerably modified by them in comparison with the common form in which it is held, and that several other doctrines of theirs are not strictly orthodox; but we have no time to follow out such a plan of exposition. We can only say that we admire the industry, temperance, neatness, systematic arrangement, and efficiency, of the clusters of Shakers which we have visited.

POETRY.

O Zion arise like a beautiful morning,
And let thy fair brightness extend far abroad;
For all shall confess it, on earth and in heaven,
That thou hast descended from none else but God;
Tho' many may rage and remonstrate against thee,
Thy holy foundation for ever shall stand
Unsullied by slander, reproach or by envy,
Upon this fair soil of America's land.

Here liberty reigns as the standard of Union,
And all are invited to gather around,
And share in the blessings prepared by heaven,
For no other good like to it can be found;
All kindreds, all colours, all nations and people,
No order or sect are rejected at all;
But all who are willing to give up their idols,
Upon this fair Zion of God they may call.

Here's a home for the widow and fatherless orphan,
A place where the wayfaring man can abide,
But all who would enter this beautiful city,
All carnal affections they must lay aside;
The ties of old nature must all be dissolved
By those who would walk in the strait narrow road;
For no carnal creature, who lives in pollution,
Can ever abide in the Zion of God.

'Then come out, Believers, and be separated
From all that's offensive to this holy cause,
And follow Christ's footsteps and live his example,
Regardless of all other precepts or laws;
'Tho' ye may meet trials, temptations and conflicts,
And sore tribulation upon you may fall,
Yet Zion shall conquer and her faithful children
Shall come off victorious over it all,

A Special Covenant of the first family of the Church Dated 3rd Month 8th 1815.

WE believe it is high time that we should come to the light, and declare our faith openly to each other, and maintain, aboveboard, what we conscientiously believe to be right, to the laying down of our lives.

I *WE do believe*, that, Father and Mother have the same spirit abiding in them, which was manifested in the first foundation pillars of the gospel, which is the only true touchstone to try all our spirits & all our ways. and only in union with their spirit and in obedience to their teaching, do we look for peace and salvation in time or eternity: Therefore, we are determined to labor for unity of spirit with them in all things, and take up our cross against that wicked nature that would lead us contrary to their counsel in any thing great or small.

It is our fixed determination to take up arms against the flesh, and war against the beast, in every shape & form that we can discover him; and for the future to avoid all unnecessary and improper intercourse with the sisters, and every thing that might have a tendency to insnare our souls or stir up any partial or ungodly affection; and labor, in the fear of God, to build up among each other the precious gifts which, from time to time, we have been taught, particularly;

1 We will not indulge ourselves in idle, vain, unprofitable or noisy conversation, or any thing of the kind, that would lead away the mind after that which is light and carnal; but we will improve our seasons of retirement in laboring for the gifts of God as we are taught.

II We will not slug about and pretend that we are unwell, when we ought to be at work, nor give way to any such spirit of idleness or carnal indulgence as would minister weakness and death to each other; but we will improve our time to the best advantage in doing good, and war against every contrary spirit & feeling as the open enemy of God and our souls.

III We will not make a god of our bellies, nor indulge a beastly appetite in any way that would clog our senses or unfit us for the exercise of any spiritual gift; nor give way to a drowsy, sleepy, sluggish sense, nor lie abed at untimely hours; for the drunkard & glutton shall come to poverty, and drowsiness shall cover a man with rags. Therefore, we will fear God and keep his com-mandments, that the shame of our nakedness do not appear.

IV We will labor to be exemplary to all our brethren and to honor the gospel in all points, as we are taught, for to this end and purpose we are called into so great a privilege; therefore, we are determined that in all our conversation and manners, and even in our very spirit and disposition we will honor our privilege, and indulge ourselves in nothing either at home or abroad, that we believe would be shameful, or wounding to the feelings of our parents; and we shall always be thankful for any orderly counsel, admonition or reproof that would help us to mortify and overcome that unruly nature that would keep us distant from our elders and obstruct the free intercourse of their lovely spirit·

V. We shall constantly labor to keep peace and harmony among each other; to avoid all envying & judging each other's gifts, and quietly labor in our own souls to shut out all evil, and keep our justification and union with the foundation, and in order to this, we shall feel ourselves under sacred obligations to confess & forsake whatever is contrary to our faith and teaching, and on no other principle to claim a lot in the family, or the privilege of uniting in the worship of God. For we do believe that without a real union of spirit with our elders and a determination to submit to their counsel, and obey them in all things, we are not justly entitled to the privileges of this family, and ought not to remain in it.

The brethren of the first order or Center family at that time, were RICHARD M'NAMER, CALVIN MORRELL SAMUEL ROLLINS, ASHBEL KITCHEL, WILLIAM SHARP, JAMES SMITH, AMOS VALENTINE ABNER BEDELL, Stephen Williams, John Dennis, John Carson, Daniel Sering, Andrew Brown Charles West, Thomas Hunt Wm Davis, Daniel Miller, Abijah Hill, Benj. Bonnel, R. Davis, R. Rankin, J. Sharp, J. Lockwood, Elias Holloway, Ezekiel Rollins, Sam-l Wallace, Moses Holloway, John Wallace & Nathan Sharp.

169601